Get Rich, Lucky Bitch

Get Rich, Lucky Bitch

A guide to creating material and spiritual wealth

DENISE DUFFIELD-THOMAS

Get Rich, Lucky Bitch

First paperback edition January 2013

For print or media interviews with Denise,
please contact info@luckybitch.com

Book design by Maureen Cutajar

ISBN-13: 978-1478181491
ISBN-10: 1478181494

www.LuckyBitch.com

This book is dedicated to YOU.

Sorting out your money dramas and daring to live a richer life will give other women permission to do the same.

And together we're going to change the world.

See you in the VIP lounge baby!

Rave Reviews from the Lucky Bitch Posse

I feel like I've truly stepped into my first class life, because of Denise's incredible teachings. I've also been able to let go of so much old stuff around money that was holding me back, and I feel like I'm truly a lucky bitch, every day of the week.

– **Nathalie Lussier**, *Digital Strategist*

I manifested an $800 scholarship to a personal growth work shop in Maui, picked up 3 new clients for my business, and $1,210 in unexpected income for the month!

– **Stephanie Dodds**, *Holistic Nutritionist*

I set a money goal that was 50% higher than any previous month – and achieved it! My other big goal was to pay off my credit card in full – which I did by the end of the course!

– **Kerry Belviso**, *Kinesiologist*

I never realized how much emotional baggage in my life was connected to money and my earning potential.

I love Denise because she's NOT all fluff – she's action-oriented and great at helping me release all my past money drama.

– **Melanie Ramiro**, *Speakers Agent & Photographer*

I manifested and closed my first 5-figure VIP client, I had NO idea about the sabotaging stories that I have been telling myself for years. I will never look at money the same again.

– **Aimee Prezzano**, *Simple Living Consultant*

I had my biggest month ever in my business earning over $4000 on my first ever e-course and having 25 women sign-up with a wait list for the next course!

– **Kathryn Hocking**, *Business Coach.*

What are YOU manifesting?
Let me know at www.LuckyBitch.com

Contents

Introduction

"Money makes the world go round"
Emcee, *Cabaret*

Hey lucky bitch!

Today is the start of your richer life - one of outrageous material and spiritual abundance (these aren't mutually exclusive by the way) and the effortless creation of your First Class life. I'm thrilled you're joining me on this journey. Because your path to riches really is a fascinating journey and I know you picked up this book because you're ready. It's time.

Pretty much my whole life I've dreamed of having enough money to do everything on my vision board and if you're reading this book, I'm guessing one of your dreams is to be wealthy too. Money *does* make the world go round, but unfortunately many women aren't getting rich because they think being rich means being a bitch (or snobby or ruthless, etc).

Collectively as a gender, we've got all these funky self-beliefs and fears about money and I wrote this book to give YOU permission to be as rich as you want.

Want to be a Serious Business Lady, swanning around the world on your personalised private jet, like a *boss*? Done.

Want to be a millionaire? Do it.

What about just having extra money to have a cleaner once a week, another holiday each year or a new car? Consider it yours.

There's no amount of money that's too big or small. You can seriously have all the abundance you want if you follow the predictable laws of the Universe. There are no exceptions. You don't have to "deserve" it. It's yours if you want it.

Helping women get out of their own way and overcome their money blocks is now my favourite hobby, as well as my life's work. And trust me, no matter where you're starting from, if you're willing to uncover what's holding YOU back, you *will* create money miracles in your life.

In return, I promise that I'll be straight up with you about what it *really* takes to uncover your true wealth and manifest money. I've been told many times that I have a knack of making complicated things seem really easy and it's because I'm really honest and frankly, I can't be bothered to bull-shit you. I'll tell you what works and what doesn't.

For many women, being rich seems like a fantasy, one that's *juuust* out of our reach or only for other women – ones that have their act together. You know, women with perfect thighs, or the perfect husband or the perfect childhood. (Spoiler alert – I have none of these things, although my husband is pretty awesome).

On the other hand, women tell me that deep down they won't ever be rich because they're afraid it would turn them into a bitch, or their friends and family won't like them anymore. That self-limiting belief is just as damaging as thinking you have to be perfect first. However, if you've got the self-awareness and you're willing to admit that only you are holding yourself back from being rich, well, that's a great start and you have everything you already need to be rich.

When I ask clients and women in my seminars about why they don't make as much money as they want, here's what I hear:

I'm just no good with money.
I've reached the limit of my earning potential.
I'm doing great; it would be greedy to want more.
I should be earning more, but I'm afraid it would cost too much (in terms of health or relationships).
My partner takes care of our money.
I'm just afraid to even look at my finances.
I wish I could just win the lottery.
Money just isn't that important to me.
I have a good life, I should just be happy with that.
I'm smart but I just can't seem to break through to the next level.

It actually doesn't matter *why* you believe you don't earn enough, because whatever you come up with is not really true and it doesn't have to be that way anymore.

I admit; I used to have a bad relationship with money. I was terrified of fully expressing my potential and I would worry what my friends and family thought about me being rich. I sabotaged myself and my career, even though I knew that I was smart and capable. I couldn't make any money from my various businesses, even though I knew that I was a born entrepreneur.

I practically *repelled* money!

But not anymore.

Now, yes, I have an amazing life. I travel whenever I like. I have world-class mentors, a great support team and I live in a $2 million penthouse overlooking a dolphin-filled harbour. But I'm still just a regular person (for some reason, I thought I'd have to change *everything* about myself to be "worthy" of success).

In full disclosure, I'm not a millionaire yet and there are many things left in my life to upgrade, but I know that it doesn't always happen over-night.

I set BIG money goals and I achieve them. Not out of fear and panic but just as a game, and I constantly work on myself so I can go to the next level. It's actually FUN to make money now, and it's fun to spend it without second guessing myself. For once in my life, I'm also surrounded by strong, powerful women who make shit-loads of money by creating good in the world. I don't have clothes with holes in them anymore. I don't walk in the rain because I can't afford a cab and I'm not cheap with myself anymore.

Guess what?

I'm no smarter than I was before. I'm no prettier, skinnier or even "luckier". I just put all my effort into overcoming my money "stuff" (all the tips that I'll share in this book) and the rest fell into place more easily than I thought possible.

So, I've spent the last three years analysing exactly what works and what doesn't in order to manifest your ideal life. I've now taught thousands of women all around the world how to use the Law of Attraction in an incredibly practical and real way that actually works. I'm not talking about airy fairy concepts about abundance. I'm saying that YOU can have more money in your pocket, feel richer on a daily basis and have a kick-ass life. Yes, YOU!

I created this book after I ran my Lucky Bitch Money Bootcamp. After the first 100 women had done the course, I knew I had created something really special because the results were incredible. Most of the women had changed their mindset *forever* and others made huge inroads every day. Word started to spread.

I started to get emails every day from women asking when I was running the next course. At first, I was planning just to run the Bootcamp a few times a year but the demand was definitely there for me to run it back to back. But I knew that not everyone could afford the tuition to change their money mindset (ironically, right?!), so I wanted to create an affordable option for women to learn the concepts I've taught about becoming wealthy. Hence this book in your hands! As you implement all the abundance tips I share, you *will* become richer and you'll probably realise exactly why you've been holding yourself back for so long.

Don't discount this book if you're already doing quite well. You've probably done a lot of personal development and you already have an abundance mindset. I also find that women who are successful are always looking for new improvements and tweaks so they can create even more abundance and satisfaction in their lives. So I know you'll get tonnes out of this book too. No matter how much money you earn, chances are you'll reach another income ceiling, and in that case, you can take everything much deeper and ask yourself, *"what else can I learn about myself?"* and of course, if you're ready for more support and an incredible group experience with other awesome women, check out www.LuckyBitch Bootcamp.com for information on the next round.

Now is the time for us as women to rise up and get rich and I'm having so much fun being a part of it. Together we're changing the world!

The path to creating your rich life can sometimes be a lonely one. Maybe you're the black sheep in your family, the only person creating success or maybe you're surrounded by rich men and you want some like-minded sisters to network and mastermind with. You're in the right place.

The Lucky Bitch posse is a powerful one and now you're a part of it. Welcome! Together our power is multiplied, so never feel like you're alone on this journey. This is a safe place to brag about your successes and share honestly about your fears.

To join the network and to get full access to your book bonuses worth almost $500, make sure you register at www.GetRichLuckyBitch.com, using the password LOVEMONEY (not case sensitive). Do it now!

Let me tell you how this all started. You might have read my first book *Lucky Bitch* which I hope has inspired you to pick up this new book. In *Lucky Bitch* I shared my secrets to becoming extraordinarily lucky and deconstructed exactly how to make the Law of Attraction work for you in the real world. It's now been read by women in more than 160 countries around the world and I get emails every day containing stories of magic, hustle and luck.

Lucky Bitch tells the story about how I became an unbelievable manifester. In the space of one year applying my secret manifesting formula (which aren't really secrets at all, more like a mix of practical actions and metaphysical techniques), I became this crazy lucky person, hence the name *Lucky Bitch*. Everything I put on my dream board came true. I just kept winning stuff and honestly, it was unbelievable, I felt like I was in a movie.

It started with little things, like winning small amounts of money at bingo (I love bingo!). Then I was given a ticket to a seminar in Vegas ($1500 value) that I had desperately wanted to attend, then a free space on a weight-loss course I thought would be life-changing for me ($200 value). Then, after setting a goal to work for myself, I happened to win a scholarship to complete a life coaching qualification, worth over $5000. Then I wanted to write a book and by "chance", I won a self-publishing home study program in a lucky door prize (over $5000 value). All these things on my goal list, all free. I didn't even become a consistent competition enterer – I just entered, and won.

Then I experienced the most amazing manifestation ever. After setting a goal to go travelling for six months, my husband and I won a travel competition with a honeymoon company to travel the world for six months staying in luxurious resorts and hotels for free. Yes you read that right, completely free and with a value of over half a million dollars. I never thought those things happened in real life and certainly not to **me**. We quit our jobs and for six months explored 12 countries and stayed in the most unbelievable places in the world. We went to New York, Kenya, Mauritius, Zanzibar, Malta, Spain, Jordan, Indonesia, Thailand, United Kingdom, Ireland and lastly, Queensland in my home country, Australia.

This trip changed my life. The thing is, we didn't just win the trip, we *consciously manifested* it. We sent constant and specific messages to the Universe that we were ready, willing, and able to leave our crappy apartment in London, throw in our jobs and take off around the world. I asked the Universe for a life changing experience and the Universe delivered! I followed my manifesting formula and amazing things happened.

I wrote *Lucky Bitch* because of that trip, and I get emails every day from women around the world, who are inspired to take their manifesting to the next level.

But the most interesting thing happened *after* the trip ended and here's where my abundance journey started. When the travel and free accommodation ended and I was sleeping on my mother's couch, I realised that even after becoming incredibly lucky, *I was still broke.* I could manifest half a million dollars' worth of free stuff, but I had never earned more than $45,000 a year in "real money". Lucky yes, but *wealthy*? …Nope.

I remember a few people had said to me during the all-expenses paid trip, *"well, what are you going to do when you have to go back to the* real *world?"*. I basically wanted to tell them to fuck off. I knew that I *was* living in the real world because I had a glimpse of what life was really like for some people. I saw how rich people vacationed. I saw how nice life could be with money, but I still had massive resistance to earning it myself and to be honest, the idea of money scared the crap out of me, even though *intellectually,* I wanted to be rich.

After the trip ended and I started out as a life coach, I remember sweating with anxiety the first time I met with an accountant about my new business. I felt like I was going to get into trouble. I was crapping myself about paying taxes before I earned my first thousand bucks. After living in 5-star hotels for six months, we were back in a small apartment in a completely different country, pretty similar to our old one. I started teaching people everything I knew about the Law of Attraction and even though I knew I had a gift, I didn't feel worthy of being a success teacher.

To be honest, I felt like the biggest fraud ever.

I did a survey to my blog subscribers at that time to ask them about their biggest goals and biggest obstacles. At least 80% of the responses mentioned **money**. They told me their fears around money; mostly that they would never have enough or earn what they felt they were worth. They spoke about their desire to live up to the potential they knew was inside them. They told me how blocked they felt and how they lay awake at night wishing things were different.

They told me how they felt like frauds when discussing money with their own clients. They told me their dreams and what they could accomplish if only they could get this "money stuff" under control. They wanted to be rich!

My first reaction was pure panic. Shit.

My next thought was, *"well, they'll have to go somewhere else for that"*.

The Universe was asking me to step up to fill this role and I was extremely reluctant, even though I knew it was a lesson I needed to learn. How could I teach something I was terrible at myself?

"Not me, Universe. Please. Don't make me do this."

But you're reading this book, so I obviously took on the challenge (otherwise, this would be a crap book, right?) and it turned out to be an even *greater* adventure than an all-expenses paid trip (and ultimately, a lot more satisfying).

I spent the next year applying everything I taught about the Law of Attraction, but this time, I applied it *directly* to my money mindset. I dealt with my fear of having money and uncovered every single money memory that was holding me back. I worked on my negative money beliefs and dug way deep down to find out why I was really scared of being rich. I examined every decision I've ever made at money and shone a light on all my mistakes. Yucky, scary work at times but oh, so worth it.

And as a result of all this work, my income doubled, then tripled. I upgraded everything in my life, slowly at first and then gained momentum. I had a few set-backs and went straight back to the simple lessons.

As a result, my income is growing every single day, and far from being a fluke, it's an easy and predictable process than anyone can learn *if* you're willing to do the self-examination.

I now teach the same principles to my private clients and in my Lucky Bitch Money Bootcamp. And now gorgeous, you'll learn them too.

I'm on a mission to change the world through helping women become rich, because I believe:

Every woman deserves to be as rich as she wants;
Every woman deserves to feel safe and taken care of;
Every woman deserves to be treated like a VIP;
Every woman deserves a First Class Life.

In *Get Rich, Lucky Bitch* you'll get the tools and inspiration you need to go to the next level of wealth. It doesn't matter if you're starting from scratch or you're itching to break through the million dollar mark, you'll realise that the only thing that's stopping you are your *current* beliefs around money. And these can be changed relatively easily when you know how. (I'm not going to bullshit you, it takes some work... but it's worth it!).

I've inspired thousands of women around the world to dream bigger and most importantly, do the practical work to manifest their dreams in the real world. You won't ever hear me say that you need to *dream harder*, in fact, I'm probably the most practical manifestation teacher you'll ever meet. You'll get day to day actions, inspiration, kick-up-the-butt real talk and the most loving advice I can give. Because I want you to be rich.

I want us to meet up in Hawaii or mastermind over cocktails in Vegas. I want us to go on charity trips together to present massive novelty sized cheques to people changing the world on the ground. I want us to go shopping together and buy things that make us feel like a million bucks. How cool would it be to say, *"Anyone up for a mastermind weekend in Cabo?"* and it just be an easy decision?

When you read books like this, it's easy to imagine the author as different to you. I've done it myself. You start to think, *"well, it's okay for* her. *Of course she has her shit together, she wrote a* book *about it"*. But I'm just a normal person. I'm not going to tell you I "cracked the code" or make you feel dumb if you don't get it.

Think of me as your sometimes bossy but usually 100% right, Virgo girlfriend and mentor. I've made tonnes of mistakes and I'm not perfect. I'm still learning how to navigate my way through life and every day I'm getting richer for it. In just a few years, I've gone from being always broke and wearing clothes literally full of holes and safety pins to living in a multi-million dollar penthouse apartment, earning awesome money, travelling the world meeting clients and feeling like life gets better each day.

Some days, I can't believe it's my life and I know I've reached about 10% of my potential. Earning money is fun now, just a game instead of being an incredibly stressful and demoralising experience. I've made probably every financial mistake possible and again, I want to reiterate: **I'm not perfect**. I'm just your everyday chick having a human experience.

Here's my other disclaimer: I'm not a financial expert. I'm not an accountant or a debt counsellor. I don't give (nor am I qualified to give) financial advice. You're not going to get spread sheets or have to do math. I'm not that kind of coach or financial advisor. I can't tell you how to invest your money or how you should pay off your debt.

However, I can honestly tell you – I've got a God-given knack for helping women like you achieve your biggest and craziest dreams. I am a mindset coach, and a fucking awesome one. (Oh yeah, and I like swearing sometimes).

Getting over your money "stuff" will help you not only earn more, but give you the confidence to pick the best, First Class team to help you invest your money. It means that you won't sabotage success or spend it all.

I've helped women cut through years of under-earning and chronic underserving, to fly through their income goals. I've helped women heal *just one* memory from their past that unlocks everything else. Decades of old self beliefs can shatter in a day and release you to earn more money. The past can heal in an instant and honestly, that's how you become rich. You're going to learn how to do that in this little book.

You'll realise it's not about the money at all.

You'll see how money is just a symbol for *everything else* in your life.

You'll discover which parts of your life need a drastic upgrade now or later, and you'll start to manifest the money to pay for it all. It's going to be fun, I promise.

So, my new best girlfriend, *are you ready?* The instant you start to second guess yourself or put the book down, I want you to forgive the mistakes you've made up until now and get excited that your world is about to change. Like, seriously, get excited, because it's finally YOUR time to manifest everything your heart desires. It's time to be wealthy, loaded, well-off, prosperous, cashed-up, well-to-do, well-heeled, bling blinged up and affluent. Whatever your version of being wealthy is, together we'll design it for you.

You are smart enough, you are ambitious enough. YOU are enough, and you deserve to be as wealthy as you want. Let's go on this amazing journey together. Let's get rich, lucky bitch!

Love, luck and abundance,
Xx Denise
Denise Duffield-Thomas
www.LuckyBitch.com

$

Becoming an Amazing Money Manifester

"The only secret of wealth creation is knowing how to use Cosmic Ordering."
Stephen Richards

I'm going to teach you how to become an amazing money manifester. It means that you'll be able to create money at will, when you want or need it *and* enjoy the process. It sounds like a big promise but I can assure you, when you follow the steps, it works. No exceptions.

Some women seem effortlessly lucky, but they are just more experienced in following the laws of the Universe. There's no magic pill and nobody is really born luckier than anyone else. It's just like how the fittest women are usually the ones who go to the gym regularly and are more consistent with their diet (lucky bitches!).

Manifesting is simply the art of transmuting a thought (a dream or a desire) into reality *in the real world* so you can touch and experience it for real. It's not just about having a great mindset. You can work on having a "millionaire mindset" but it doesn't always translate into actual dollars in your bank account. Learning how to manifest money follows the same predictable process.

When I read and watched the world-wide phenomenon, *The Secret*, I thought it was amazing, but I was totally confused about what to *do*. Like, do I just meditate on what I want? Do I have to wish really, *really*, REALLY hard and my life will change? Will I win the lottery if I think about it all day long?

I was obviously doing it wrong because I was still broke. Incredibly frustrating to say the least and I felt like an idiot, calling myself a self-professed "personal development junkie" but not being able to make it work.

Like many ambitious, entrepreneurial women, I went on a journey of self-discovery to try and find the secret to money. I walked on hot coals with Tony Robbins; I went to countless personal development seminars, listened to dodgy internet marketing salesmen selling me their "System to Riches", and tried to push through my blockages with sheer will power.

I loooooved talking about money in the abstract sense and devoured any book with "millionaire" in the title, but again I want to reiterate, I was broke. I was in tens of thousands of dollars in debt but more importantly, I completely and repeatedly sabotaged my earning potential, so I was a money *repellent*.

Now, this isn't one of those stories where I say I was homeless on the street, stealing T.Vs for crack money and then I turned it all around. I was just your everyday chick, earning an okay salary in a corporate job, with a couple of credit cards and personal loans and a fairly hefty overdraft. I lived paycheck to paycheck. I could afford to feed and clothe myself, lived an okay life but I *felt* poor.

Like you, I didn't want to be *ordinary*. I didn't want to live in my small, cramped flat in the outskirts of town with

Ikea furniture. I didn't want to walk to work in the rain, or worry about paying the bills. Most of all, I didn't want to be dependent on *anyone* for money, especially not a man.

I wanted to be RICH. I wanted to walk into a fancy store and wear awesome clothes. I wanted more than one pair of black shoes and one winter coat. I wanted to vacation as often as I wanted and I wanted to prove to the world I could make a huge impact and get rewarded for it monetarily. While my friends were climbing the corporate ladder, I spent my time going to conferences and reading abundance books, but I felt like there was a missing puzzle piece. There *must* have been something I was missing.

The *idea* of manifesting was awesome, but as a practical Virgo, I needed to know the specifics and the logistics. What should I do next? *And then what?* Is there an order I should follow? Am I doing it "right"? *Where's my money?*

Don't worry. You don't need to follow a complicated system, or learn to meditate really well. I figured it out for you, so you can just relax and follow the process.

As a coach and mentor to thousands of ambitious and entrepreneurial women around the world, I'm asked questions like this...

Denise – what affirmations are the best?
What's the right way to make a dream board?
How should I word my goals?
How many times a day should I write them out?
Which works better, EFT or Access Consciousness?
Do subliminal CDs really work?

Here's the answer. Try it all. It ALL WORKS. My philosophy is *throw everything at it*. It's your life and your dreams deserve to be fulfilled no matter what it takes.

You'll hear personal development gurus say that *their* book, system or process is the only right way, but that's bullshit. There's no perfect way to word your affirmations, there's not the definitive dream board software. Everything compounds and helps you achieve your goals; you just have to be consistent and persistent in your achievement of wealth.

Of course, just doing random stuff willy-nilly doesn't work either, there's definitely a flow you should follow. My manifesting process isn't the only way but I know it *works* – not just from my own life, but from the awesome women I coach on a daily basis who create miracles and make progress faster than the average women, even the ambitious ones who grit their teeth and try *really* hard. Trust me; it doesn't have to be that hard.

Don't get too caught up in one particular tool being the silver bullet that will change everything. Even this book.

All the personal development tools work, but it will take more than one thing, *done only once* to activate the Law of Attraction. What we're doing is ripping holes through time and space. We're literally rearranging the Universe in your favour. You don't need a magic wand or a Tardis to shift the Universe, but it's not going to happen by wishing on a star one night either.

I'm not going to bullshit you. Becoming a conscious manifester requires you to *practice* and honestly, most people don't have the discipline to practice to get good. It's not going to be effortless straight away, just like learning any worthwhile skill. I can't be fucked learning to play the piano because I don't have any patience to learn or practice. I would love to be a good singer, but I've got a shitty voice and it seems too hard to take lessons and learn to be good at it. Manifesting is the same way, yet, a lot of people get pissed that it doesn't work the first time. Spoiler alert - you might not manifest a million bucks the first time you try. (Good, I think I've just lost the time-wasters… everyone else, read on!)

When I was manifesting my goal of travelling for six months, I tried *everything*, *every day*. I did it all - visualising, goal setting, tapping, journaling, forgiving, dream boards, etc to make that dream into reality. The Universe had an interesting way of bring the opportunity to me, but I wasn't trying to manifest a competition. I just wanted to go travelling.

Every day, I made at least 10-20 little subtle shifts to tell the Universe I was deadly serious about wanting to travel the world for six months with Mark, before I even knew about the travel competition. I got obsessed with my goal.

All up, I estimated I tried more than 50 personal development tips and tools to manifest that goal. For the real specifics, I encourage you to read *Lucky Bitch* as well as this book. It's an awesome story, but it also shows how consistent you need to be when you're consciously manifesting a life out of the ordinary. That's why most people live a life of mediocrity, always settling for an economy class life and never setting or reaching big income goals. For most people, they are just not willing to put in the work to live an extraordinary life, just like I'm not willing to put in the effort required to become an amazing singer.

I know you are different and you're reading this book and following the steps because you have that burning desire and you're willing to do what it takes.

"The most popular labour-saving device is still money."
Phyllis George

Honestly, most people are pretty passive and let life happen, vaguely hoping for a lottery win to get them out of their financial reality.

I'm not criticising. I've done it myself.

Some months, I set a really big financial goal and do everything in my power to make it happen. Other times, I just wish money would fall into my lap. It's human and it's normal. But acknowledge that you're doing it to yourself.

In between manifesting big goals, I find myself getting lazy and letting some of my daily manifesting activities slide. So, in response, the Universe gets really lazy and slow about manifesting my goals. Some days it is SO easy to manifest money, it's flying in so fast that I'm amazed. Then I'll get lazy and think I can skip a day or two of my manifesting exercises. After a while, the fear sets in and the money dries up. It happens every time and when you follow the process (or not), the results are fairly predictable.

The gym analogy really is perfect here - when you're in the zone with your exercise, it feels easy and when you've been procrastinating going to the gym, it feels sooooo hard to go back.

So, it might sound like a lot of hard work and frenzied activity to *actively* manifest your ideal life and become rich, but once you've read this book, you'll see there are a few key shifts you need to make, and then the rest are the little subtleties that will grow your income even further. Once that happens, it becomes a fun game.

There's no doubt that manifesting requires patience and constant vigilance to stay positive and in the right frame of mind. But once you have the hang of it and start to see the results, you get quicker and stronger, and it becomes self-fulfilling. Just like your body has muscle memory, each time you get to a new phase of money consciousness, even if you backslide and go back to old habits, just follow the system again and you'll get back on track easily.

The Money Manifesting Formula

In a nutshell, here is my 5-step formula for manifesting anything, including money:

1. Declutter everything in your life
2. Decide exactly what you want
3. Surround your life with positivity
4. Take inspired action
5. Receive and fine-tune

This formula can be used to manifest literally *anything* in your life. I teach it in my Money Bootcamp, my Soul Mate course and every single other course. Literally, you could read this book again and substitute "love" or "weight" for money and get incredible results. It doesn't matter if the goal is HUGE or tiny. You can use this formula to manifest your next car, a new job, 5 new clients by Thursday, your future husband, *anything*.

I've used this formula with clients to help them manifest things like:

- a positive court case outcome
- $5000 within 48 hours
- a husband and a baby within a year for a client who was single for 7 years

- a dream dance job on a cruise ship
- a new dream house in record time
- a quick house sale to avoid foreclosure
- forgiveness with a family member

With practice using the formula you will start to receive what you ask for, even money. Simple as that. You don't have to be incredibly smart or particularly lucky to follow it – it just takes practice.

The best thing is that you won't just manifest "stuff", like when I started winning scholarships and prizes. When you follow the steps with a particular focus on money, it will become effortless. Money will start coming in from everywhere. I know it, because I've witnessed it with my Money Bootcamp participants and it's unbelievable how the money starts rolling in.

When I write a new book or course, I write down the five steps of the manifesting formula and design it with that flow in mind. When I'm stuck on my own goals, I just go back and mentally check off the steps, to make sure I'm not missing anything.

It's also designed as a circle. When you get to step five and your goal hasn't manifested yet, go back to step one and start again. There's always more to declutter, always more to clear, you can get even *more* specific, you can take more inspired action and you can practice the art of allowing more abundance to come into your life. It seriously works every time if you follow it.

Each step contains many different practical and metaphysical exercises, which we'll cover in this book. If you want to go further, I've got some life changing resources for you, so make sure you register at www.GetRichLuckyBitch.com.

Remember, this isn't a university assignment. It's not some massive test you have to pass. You don't have to be a certain weight, colour, age or profession for this to work. It works for everyone.

When it came to manifesting success and especially money, I had my own self-limiting beliefs. I thought I'd have to become a completely different person - certainly a skinnier, nicer, more organised and "perfect" person. But I'm here to tell you - **YOU ARE ALLOWED TO BE RICH**, no matter who you are. Sorry to shout, but I want you to get this. You don't have to wait until some mythical time in the future. You can be ready NOW. Got that girlfriend?

My manifesting formula is not an intellectual exercise. The thing with the Law of Attraction is that just thinking it is not enough. You have to *feel* it and every cell in your body has to believe it. You have to get into the space of living abundantly before the means to live abundantly actually shows up in your world. You might have to fake it at first but that's okay, because it still works!

> *"When Riches begin to come, they come so quickly and in such great abundance that one wonders where they have been hiding during all those lean years"*
> Napoleon Hill

I remember reading that quote, and I was like *"but WHEN, mutherfucker?!"* I was sooo impatient, but when I look at the manifesting formula, I really wasn't following the steps. I was the equivalent of sitting on the couch eating donuts and being frustrated I wasn't skinny. Exact same thing.

Winning that round-the-world trip was the turning point for my belief in my own manifesting power. Since then I have continued to manifest amazing things from my dream board. Every time I break through an income goal, I go back to step one and work through the barriers to the next stage. I don't have any magical power, I just work the steps, exactly how you will. These strategies have worked for women all around the world. I've shared my manifesting secrets with more than 42,000 women from 169 countries and more women are breaking through their own limits every day. It will work for you too.

My manifesting formula provides you with practical techniques to start bringing more actual money into your life (not just about teaching you how to win competitions and lucky door prizes). Be open to receiving money in your life, not just about being really lucky.

It doesn't matter where you're starting from, whether you grew up rich or poor, we're going to unravel all of your complicated money stuff and clean the slate so you can create a new healthy money relationship and get some cash in the bank.

By the end of this book you will have set some non-scary but exciting financial goals, you'll know which way you're headed and what you need to do to achieve the wealth you want. We'll remove all of the hurdles on your path to being rich. We've got some "Denise Real Talk" on dealing with negative people, self-sabotaging behaviour and some of the snags on your road to financial awesomeness. I promise you uncensored truth bombs on what it really takes.

I'll show you how to take back your power around money in all situations and learn to be cool and safe as a rich woman. I'll share inspiring stories of normal women just like you who got more open to receiving money and on their way to becoming rich. You're in great company.

So really, manifesting is such a simple, predictable process, even though it deals with metaphysical concepts like manipulating time and space to your will, becoming a reverse paranoid (believing that the whole world is conspiring to help you) and doing some, quite frankly, weird rituals.

It doesn't really matter if you believe in the Law of Attraction or think it's a pile of new age poop. It still works. I've worked with some total sceptics who tried to convince me that they were different and so fucked up that it wouldn't work for them. It does and it will for you too.

Just follow the steps.

Are you ready?

Chapter Summary

- Manifesting is the art of transmuting a thought into reality in the real world
- Manifesting Formula Recap
    - Declutter everything in your life
    - Decide exactly what you want
    - Surround your life with positivity
    - Take inspired action
    - Receive and fine-tune

  If something isn't manifesting quickly enough, you've probably skipped a step.
- Throw everything at it – it's your dream life after all!

$

Your First Manifesting Assignment

"There are people who have money and people who are rich."
Coco Chanel

Ready to put the formula into practice? Before you can start to take the reins of a multi-million dollar fortune, you need to get intimate with what's already in your life. You might think *"hey I already know my money, I haven't got enough!"*

Trust me, this might be the case for now, but to get yourself ready for more, you've got to be a good steward of every penny, cent or dime that comes into your life. It's a really important lesson and one that has truly changed my life, and the way I feel about money.

Acknowledge Every Cent

This will truly change how you feel about money and attract more to you like a magnet. Let me tell you a harsh truth: you can't manifest money when you feel broke.

You might think I'm missing the point. After all, why would you be reading this book if you already had all the money you needed? But that's the frustrating paradox of the Law of Attraction. You will only get *more* of what you've already got.

With this exercise, we're starting to train your awareness. Every woman I coach is WAY more abundant than she actually thinks and I bet you a hundred bucks that you're exactly the same. Seriously, if I'm wrong, send me a hundred bucks.

Here's the exercise - every day write down a list of all of the money that comes into your life. Track every cent, whether it's from salary, gifts, money in the street, bonuses or an inheritance. Big or small, track it every single day and most importantly, feel good about it.

By paying close attention to all those extra little bits and pieces of money that comes your way you will start to activate the Law of Attraction. Remember, like attracts like. So the more money you realise you have, the more money will start flowing to you. On the other hand, if you focus on how you lack money in your life, you literally send the Universe poor vibrational energy and attract much of the same thing - which isn't money! That's why when you're feeling really broke, you end up getting unexpected bills in the post or you get a speeding fine. You just attract more misfortune.

It's also good to track everything else of value that comes into your life that might not be actual money. It could be gifts, savings/discounts, or it could be things that you receive for free. By taking note of these things you might realise you actually get more free stuff than money, so you might need to switch your focus to manifest more money.

Remember how I said I used to win things all the time? I only realised the disparity when I started to track my money. When I saw that I manifested more than half a million dollars' worth of freebies in a year and only £30,000 of actual *income,* I knew it was time for a change. No, I wasn't looking a gift horse in the mouth; I wanted the experience of actually *paying* for things myself. I knew I wanted to go to the next level of wealth.

Make a commitment to track your money every single day for at least a month because *what gets measured gets improved*. It's just one of the laws of the Universe.

"The person who doesn't know where his next dollar is coming from usually doesn't know where his last dollar went."
Unknown

When I stop recording and tracking my money daily, I manifest less of it. I start to get freaked out about my money goals for the month. When I track it every day, I make more. I'm excited about my abundance and appreciate every cent that comes in. Money is attracted to me. Simple.

You'll start to be surprised how much comes into your life unexpectedly and how much you discount your current level of abundance. The Universe doesn't appreciate being ignored.

You don't have to have fancy spread sheets or know your profit and loss. Just start with tracking everything that comes in on a simple piece of paper or a Google spread sheet. You can get apps for it. It really doesn't matter how.

Don't think you can only start when you have a "perfect" system. That doesn't exist and it's just procrastination disguised as the need to be organised. Start with a simple sheet of paper, or get your free beautiful money tracking sheet from www.GetRichLuckyBitch.com.

It doesn't have to be scary or confusing to deal with your money. Just know how much money you're already manifesting so you can attract more.

"I'm so naive about finances. Once when my mother mentioned an amount and I realized I didn't understand, she had to explain: 'That's like three Mercedes.' Then I understood."
Brooke Shields

Tracking your money is incredibly important if you've had frustration over not hitting a financial goal. Chances are you already hit it and didn't even realise, which makes you seem incredibly ungrateful to the Universe. Why give you more if you can't even acknowledge what you're getting?

Kerry Belviso, a kinesiologist on my bootcamp told me, *"I realised that I only feel that money that comes through my account is "real", so I disregard money in my PayPal account, or money that comes as cash (even though it is recorded for tax purposes)"*.

This feeling of money not being "real" is what derails most women from feeling truly rich. When we discount income or abundance "that doesn't really count", we're actually PUSHING away more money.

Kat Loterzo, a fat loss expert had no idea she was already hitting her big income goals, *"I started doing my money tracking sheet, with a goal to manifest $20,000 or more this month. I finally went and backdated every cent received so far in August... and I've already passed the halfway mark. I had no idea!"*

Kerrie and Kat's stories are not uncommon. Women are notoriously bad at acknowledging themselves and as a gender; we suck at claiming our power around money. The act of tracking money daily has increased Kat's income more than double than before she did the Bootcamp. Best of all, it's doing something she loves - helping women lose weight. She had the skills before, she just didn't realise how she was holding herself back from being paid beautifully for it.

Tracking simply gives you the information to hit, exceed and adjust your goals as you get better at manifesting and keeping money.

If I had to ask you how much you earned last year, last quarter, last month... would you be able to tell me? *Honestly*?

"I don't want to make money,
I just want to be wonderful."
Marilyn Monroe

When I started working with my own money mentor, Kendall Summerhawk, I was too afraid to ask her a question in case she asked me how much money I made. I honestly had no idea! It was awesome when just six months later I stood up at a microphone at her annual money conference and proudly told her I earned $17,000 that month. For the first time in my life, I actually tracked it and wasn't scared about it. It allowed me to grow it each and every month.

Honestly, tracking played a huge part in allowing me to increase my income. It will for you too, so starting today, track everything.

Frequently Asked Questions

I get more questions about this exercise than any of the more complicated ones! I understand you want to get it right, but it's pretty simple. Any type of tracking is going to be better than none.

Do I track my partner's income?

Yes and no. **No** if you're reading this book so you can learn to manifest for yourself. A lot of women are awesome manifesters... for other people. For example, you set a money goal, and then your partner gets a pay increase or inheritance. That's just another form of hiding out from money. If you are attracting money *through* your partner, then for the next few months, ONLY track what comes to you alone. That way you can adjust accordingly and focus on receiving abundance for YOU.

Yes you can track his income too if you want to work with your partner to create even more abundance as a couple. You could always encourage them to track for themselves too, especially if you like some healthy competition. See who is best at manifesting their income goals each month. Have a competition to see who can find the most money in the street!

Should I track expenses as well?

I'm a big fan of knowing what you're spending, so if you already track your expenses, keep doing it. Your main focus right now should be on what you bring IN to give awareness to your money manifesting ability. That doesn't mean go crazy on your budget and spend more than you earn. It just means for this book and in my courses, focus on what you want to grow. It's unrealistic for you to try a million exercises all at once, so if you're picking one simple thing to do – track your incoming money first.

Remember I'm not a debt counsellor or a financial planner. My focus is on improving your mindset around money and helping you feel rich.

Do I really need to track everything?

Yes, everything that comes into your life.

So when you find a penny in the street, pick it up, kiss it and say, "thank you, Universe", then track it! I'm totally not above picking up money in the street, I love it!

For how long should I track my money?

Forever. Do it every day, even if you are earning very little or multi-millions. This amazingly simple habit can take you into riches. Even my multi-million dollar mentors track their money every day, maybe they just switch to daily totals rather than tracking each sale individually, but they still know what they make, almost to the penny.

Chapter Summary

- Track everything, every single cent. Tracking shows the Universe you're paying attention to the abundance already in your life.
- To help you with your first assignment, I've created some bonus tracking sheets for you. Print them out and have fun updating them every day with every bit of money that comes into your life.

Get your free tracking sheets from
www.GetRichLuckyBitch.com

$

Can Everyone Really Be Rich?

"Money without brains is always dangerous."
Napoleon Hill

Barbara Streisand once said "success is having ten honeydew melons and eating only the top half of each one", isn't that awesome? She truly is a rich, successful and accomplished woman.

However, the above quote from Napoleon implies that only smart people should be rich. From my research on women and money, that's not true at all. I know many highly intelligent, funny, talented and generous women who are broke. I've seen people grow rich on "dumb luck" and every shade in between. So, how do we know what qualities are shared by truly rich women?

For our purposes, we can look at celebrity women. Why?

You might not know anyone who has won the lottery, and you might only know a handful of truly wealthy people, so celebrities are a handy example of what happens when people get rich quickly and sometimes unexpectedly. Although celebrities are usually above average in the looks department, they are probably just as intelligent as you and me, so we can learn a lot from them.

However, most of the celebrity headlines at the moment seem to be about babies (has it always been this way or is my biological clock particularly sensitive about this?) and you rarely hear a celebrity talk about money. You can look up the fact that Julia Roberts got $20 million for *Oceans 11*, the cast of *Friends* negotiated together for a million an episode and Elizabeth Taylor was the first actress to break the million dollar pay check but how often do you hear celebrities actually talk about how they *spend* or save it and what actually happens when you're so rich you literally couldn't spend it all. I would love to hear Oprah talk about what it's like to open her bank statements, or ask Meryl Streep about her investments. It would be fascinating, right?

Lessons from Rich and Poor Celebrities

Some celebrities just hum along amassing huge fortunes and others get it and lose it just as quickly. Did you know that Judge Judy has made $45 million from her syndicated court room show? It hasn't changed much over the years, maybe she's got a slightly fancier robe, but she's the highest-paid person on television and the 13th richest woman in entertainment, according to *Forbes*. She earns more from her T.V. gig than Simon Cowell and David Letterman. Who knew?!

When I went researching for rich celebrities, I found only two types of information. The first was announcements of large movie-star pay checks, often not validated by the celebrities themselves (and apparently a bit of a P.R. move) and then page after page of bankruptcies and sad stories about celebs blowing it all.

I guess it's boring to report the good news and it's really rare to hear a celeb brag about their lifestyle (except on Cribs, I guess, but they aren't talking about actual cash) or talk about their income at all. They seem to be very shy on the topic.

I found plenty of cautionary tales though.

From ThisIsMoney.co.uk:

"A £90k wedding, 15 pairs of designer Ugg boots and luxury holidays": How Tina Malone's Shameless spending made her bankrupt.

The star of the UK's T.V. show *Shameless* tells how she's a sucker for sob stories and her "over the top generosity" in buying gifts for friends and taking her family on all-expenses paid holidays led her to bankruptcy.

It's the exact same tale we hear when someone blows their lottery winnings. She earns £100,000 a year, not an astronomical sum in the celebrity world but she spends it as if she's a millionaire. It's easy to judge her but it's a common tale that stops women from being wealthy - being over generous. More on that in a moment.

Have you heard of the pop singer Limahl? Nope, neither had I until I saw him featured in a "celebrity money story" on the Telegraph website. He was friends with Elton John in the 70s and blew all his cash before his pop career fizzled out. The feast and famine cycle is incredibly common for celebrities and normal people alike.

Some one-hit wonders rake in the cash for years,

others spend it just as quickly as their song was in the charts. The number one song the day I was born, *My Sharona* by The Knack still makes guitarist/songwriter Berton Averre an awesome amount of money in radio, television and movie royalties.

"It is far and away the major part of my income stream, and somehow it just keeps going strong," he told ninemsn in an unusually candid interview about money. To be fair, it's an awesome song, but it's unusual to hear about how people make their money.

Korean pop sensation Psy has made over $8 million dollars from *Gangnam Style* at the time of writing (it's probably more now). If he's careful, he can turn that one-hit wonder into a sizable nest egg or he can blow it on lavish spending like M.C Hammer, who burnt through his $30 million dollar fortune quickly on an expensive entourage and outrageous spending. Funny that the two performed together at the 2012 American Music Awards with a Gangnam Style / 2 Legit 2 Quit mash up. Maybe M.C gave him some financial advice in the green room?

Hope this is not depressing, but would you like more examples of celebrity money gone bad?

Anna Nicole Smith was thisclose to getting a Gold Digger's Hall of Fame entry from her billionaire husband but died broke. Cautionary tale - don't marry old dudes for money. It's not the best financial plan in the world.

Patricia Kluge, who at one point set the record for the largest divorce settlement ever, got through a reported billion dollars on large gaudy jewellery, paintings and vineyards. Lesson – keep some money for a rainy day.

Kim Basinger filed for bankruptcy in 1983 after a $20 million dollar commercial real estate deal went south and

Main Line Pictures sued her for backing out of *Boxing Helena*. Lesson - don't overextend yourself in the good times... and get a good lawyer to get you out of shitty movies.

Remember the gorgeous Tia Carrere from *Wayne's World*? She was also starring in *General Hospital* at the time and filed for bankruptcy so she could get out of the contract and into movies. She lost the suit and have you seen her in much recently? Lesson - don't piss off the head honchos.

Nadya "Octomom" Suleman is doing soft-core porn now to pay her bills. Lesson - don't have 14 children if you can't afford it.

What about Toni Braxton? She should be as famous (and rich) as Mariah Carey and Celine Dion, and she's certainly as talented but she's filed for bankruptcy *twice* due to excessive spending, divorce and illness. When you think how much money Mariah makes on her Christmas covers *alone*, it's sad to hear that Toni ended up so broke. She had to sell her personal possessions including awards she had received, when she should be making more music and living off her royalties. Lesson - I don't know - get a pre-nup and better health insurance?

I'm not being a glib bitch here. We actually have no idea how these celebrities lost all their money and it's easy to judge from the outside.

Duchess Sarah Ferguson, Courtney Love, La Toya Jackson, Judy Garland, Kerry Katona, Pamela Anderson, Mischa Barton, Amy Winehouse, Lindsay Lohan, the list of women who seemingly blew entire fortunes on shopping, bad divorces, alcohol, drugs and lavish lifestyles goes on and on. Looks like celebrities, with all their money, connections and good looks aren't any better with their money than the average population. Why not?

If you were to ask them, they'd probably say that their finances were mismanaged by their financial team or stolen by their parents. That the economy affected them as much as the average woman. That they gave it away to friends and family who took advantage of their generosity. That a million bucks doesn't go very far these days. Most of them would probably say they have *no idea* how it happened. Just like most of us when we're in debt or have no money at the end of the month. Seriously, *where did it all go?*

How about we sum them all up with one blanket diagnosis – **self sabotage.**

Although the list of celebrity bankruptcies is larger for men, we know that women don't earn as much as men in the first place. These women don't have much in common – some were born rich, some poor. They are different ethnicities and have varying degrees of talent. You could say that being in the public eye doesn't help you stay rich but take an average neighbourhood and you'll find plenty of similar stories, just on a different scale.

Even though the sums are different, I'm guessing the same issues that plague celebrities are the same stuff that holds you back from hitting the six figure mark in your business, from keeping more of your income and from living the life you've always wanted. Piling more money on top doesn't deal with the underlying money issues. That's why I hate when people email me in desperation asking how to win the lottery. It might sound like an awesome solution but chances are, it would be gone quickly for the same reasons as why they are broke now.

Should you give money away?

Being overly generous is something that plagues many women. What should feel good becomes an overwhelming need to be liked. What starts off as charitable turns into being bled dry. I believe in the power of giving, but when it comes at your own personal cost, it becomes self-sabotage.

I'm not even talking about charitable giving. Are you always the first (or only) person to reach for the restaurant bill? Do you lend money and never ask for it to be paid back? Do you feel overly responsible for other people's money dramas?

You might not be supporting an entourage of friends and family members like some celebrities but being too generous is often a disguise for your inability to receive from others. Giving shouldn't bankrupt you. Giving shouldn't block more abundance to you or keep others from learning their own financial lessons. Don't leave yourself a victim by over-giving, make sure your giving feels good and still honours *you* first and your financial goals.

When it comes to lending money to friends and family, follow Suze Orman's advice. Don't loan money if you've got credit card debt yourself, prepare a written contract for repayment and don't do it to enable someone else's poor money management.

"Men and women both have an equal capacity to make money, but they want money for different reasons. Men want money for power and women want it for comfort, and usually not their own comfort, but the comfort of others in their lives."

Suze Orman

By the way, I saw Suze Orman speak at a Hay House conference and she started her speech with "I stand before you a very very *very* wealthy woman". I loved it, so inspiring to see a woman completely owning her power. I hope to stand on stage one day and say the same thing. Suze understands that a lot of women feel scared about money and I really highly recommend her books.

Suze says, *"Don't panic. When the topic turns to money, so many women fall into a horrible default mode of* "I can't do this" *or* "I don't know what to do." *I want you to commit to one month of telling yourself,* "Yes, I can." *That crucial change in attitude is the first step."*

Who are you trying to impress?

What about keeping up with the Jones's (or the Elton Johns in the case of pop-star Limahl)?

Who do you try to impress with your money? Are there people in your life who you feel inferior to? Do you ever go on lavish shopping sprees you can't afford in order to feel good about yourself?

This one can be so tempting because we have access to so much cheap credit. Although I live in an incredible (rented) apartment, I have a fairly shitty car. I've had a few people tell me I should get a loan to get something more flashy. I am saving for a new car so I can pay for it in cash, like my current one. I only use it a few times a week as I work from home, so I'd only be getting a loan to impress other people. I can tell you from experience how expensive it can be to impress people. It took us three years to pay off our wedding, which we couldn't really afford, because we wanted to impress our friends and family. It's a common sabotage and probably the easiest to fall into.

Let's talk guilt and money. I've heard from two separate friends that a sizable inheritance made them feel so guilty that they blew it within weeks. One friend got a huge payout after her brother died of cancer and the money made her feel *sick*. She blew it on a few holidays that she didn't even enjoy.

The sad story of 9/11 widow Kathy Trant is a classic case of guilt sabotage. She received $5 million dollars in insurance payouts for the death of her husband Dan, who worked on the 104th floor of the World Trade Centre. According to the *New York Post,* she spent $2 million on home repairs, more than $500,000 to take friends and relatives on cruises and holidays, gave friends sums of $20,000 and $15,000 to pay debts and buy real estate, and bought two women boob jobs (one a beauty therapist she had just met). It's a heart-breaking story because the money was frittered away on largely meaningless things, leaving her broke and of course, still grief-stricken. Can you imagine being in the same situation, how hard it would be to enjoy that money, knowing where it came from and why?

I've personally seen people get large windfalls of money only to blow it all on over-the-top presents for their kids, inappropriate toys they can't afford to maintain or by giving it away to others. It didn't bring them any long-lasting joy or security. As tempting as the fantasy is, winning the lottery or getting a huge cash injection won't solve anything. It's self-sabotage, pure and simple.

One last example from the celebrity cautionary tales – giving up responsibility to others. This one has ruined many a celeb and can be a huge warning to a lot of women.

Remember TLC? Their album *CrazySexyCool* sold 10 million copies, but the girls had to declare bankruptcy soon after because their contract meant they earned very little after everyone else was paid.

Rihanna has filed a lawsuit against her former accountants who apparently took 22% of her tour revenues, while she earned less than 6%. The firm represented her from age 16 til when she finally fired them in 2010.

American Idol winner Fantasia almost lost her home to foreclosure. In her autobiography she admitted she was functionally illiterate and was unable to read her contracts. She trusted her management to act in her best interest.

Yoko Ono sued EMI for $10 million, claiming she was cheated out of royalties from John Lennon's estate. In June 2012, Lauryn Hill pleaded guilty to tax evasion and faces a three year jail sentence.

Reality star Kate Gosselin accused her ex-husband of stealing all the money in their joint bank account leaving her broke, despite all her reality T.V show money.

Annie Leibovitz got into $24 million in debt, mostly from unpaid taxes, property deals and an incomplete book deal. She had to sell off many of her original photographs to get back on track.

Other women who claim bad management, that other people cheated them out of their money or who were screwed over by ex-partners - Lindsay Lohan, Courtney Love (those two again!), Britney Spears, Anne Heche, Kelis and former *Happy Days* star Erin Moran. Nothing is ever mentioned or admitted about bad financial management, poor decision making, excessive shopping or drugs and alcohol. They trusted others to make their decisions for them or put their head in the sand. Seriously, even though the sums are different – how many of have done the same?

In Britney's 2008 divorce papers, it showed that she spent practically all of her $737,000 monthly income (yes, that's *monthly* income). It went mostly on rental properties for her and her family, entertainment and restaurants. Yes, she'll still get royalties for years to come but what happens when it dries up? How many of us live pay-check to pay-check? We think that if we earned more money, that problem would be solved, but it wouldn't. Even though we don't earn as much as Britney, the default behaviour is the same, right?

What about something just as dangerous?

In her book *Nice Girls Don't Get Rich,* Lois P. Frankel cites giving away power, especially to men and other authority figures as one of the main reasons that women don't get rich. Unfortunately, we're often taught at a young age to believe the men in our lives know more about money than we do and many women feel scared and intimidated in talking about it. Lois says *"don't relinquish your say in financial matters in order to avoid bruised egos. If you do, you only lengthen the time it takes you to become financially free"*. By the way, her book is excellent and I highly recommend adding it to your financial success library.

It doesn't matter how powerful or rich we view the celebrity; they aren't immune to giving away their power either. I found several quotes that made me go "hmmm". I was searching the Telegraph.co.uk's regular celebrity money feature and found these interesting nuggets.

From self-proclaimed "rich chav" Jordan aka Katie Price, the Page 3 topless model and now empire builder:

"Are you a saver or a spender?"
"I spend but I have people around me who save for me. My brother and another guy look after my money. I don't know what I've got. At least I don't know to the penny what I've got."

And Australia's own Olivia Newton John:

"Do you use a financial adviser?"
"Well, I have a wonderful husband, John, who's a businessman. I feel more comfortable turning to him. He has my best interests at heart and I trust him. He's very knowledgeable and I've learnt a lot from him about running my business interests and my finances."

This celebrity feature isn't to make fun of anyone; we're using these as cautionary (and extreme) examples of what normal women do too. Basically - they are just like us - just with higher incomes and greater extremes. They spend beyond their means, rarely save money, give away their power to men in their lives, and make bad money decisions. Celebrities - they're just like us!

I've heard the same thing many times from real-life women:

- *It's too confusing for me*
- *It's easier if he manages it*
- *I don't know where my money goes*
- *I don't know the first thing about money*
- *I'm always broke at the end of the month*
- *I hate dealing with the bills*
- *I have no idea how much debt we have*
- *Money stresses me out too much*

- *I don't open my credit card statements*
- *I just need more money, that would solve everything*

So how can you learn the lessons from these celebs and not make the same mistakes?

Don't worry or get depressed. There are a lot of positive examples of awesome rich women with healthy relationships with money and we'll cover them in this book, but we'll also look at *why* we're acting this way and how we can give up the sabotaging behaviour to have a beneficial and abundant relationship with money, no matter how rich we get.

You know that annoying quote that every personal development guru spouts: "*the definition of insanity is doing the same thing over and over again and expecting a different result*", or as my husband Mark puts it, "*the definition of insanity is hearing the same quote over and over again*".

Well – in this case, it's true. It's ridiculous for anyone to expect their financial circumstances to change without changing the behaviour that got them there in the first place. That's why I'm glad you bought this book. It's a great first start into living a richer life. However, it's just the start. Learning to become rich is a life-long process for some people and one that will require you to ruthlessly declutter everything in your life (mainly beliefs and self-sabotaging behaviours) that's not working and constantly examine *why* you're acting the way you do. It's about giving up the victim mentality and accept that only YOU are responsibility or to "blame". Are you willing to do what it takes?

I'm not making fun of any of these celebrity women, I'm actually incredibly grateful that we can learn from them (especially if you don't personally know any rich women in your own life). I didn't know any wealthy women at all. I didn't know how to act with money, except what I saw on T.V and in movies. Honestly, there aren't many good role models out there, so I see that we lucky bitches have a responsibility.

You don't need to become famous to be rich, and I'm not going to ask you to rob a bank or do anything unethical in order to become rich, but this first step - uncovering and then decluttering what's holding you back, can be tough for some people. In fact, I spend about 80% of my work with clients and Lucky Bitch Money Bootcamp participants in this step, but it can be uncomfortable.

It can be tough to admit that you sabotage your money by giving away your power to the men in your life, overspend on shopping or being overly generous but the self-awareness is the key to breaking free of old habits and allowing yourself to receive more.

The good news is that it's also incredibly freeing and transformational. When you get rid of everything between your ears that's not conducive to earning money and then follow the rest of the manifesting formula, it becomes (gasp) *easy*.

No joke.

I've seen it myself with all the clients I work with and in my own life. For YEARS, I tried to work for myself. I was a born entrepreneur but I never earned any money for it. Yes, a dollar here and there, but nothing serious. Definitely not enough to quit my job, which I desperately wanted to do.

The month I decided to work on absolutely decluttering my life of every negative money belief and fear, I made $225 in my business.

Not impressed? Ok, that's not that exciting. However - this is more than I made in *18 months* of one of my "practice businesses" on the side of my full time job. I celebrated every penny of that $225, because I knew it was just the start. It finally felt easy and fun, and I wasn't afraid anymore (until I hit my next money barrier but that's further along in this book).

I had more decluttering to go, so I made it a game. The more I cleared, the more money I made. In fact, I doubled my income in the second month ($450), then doubled it again ($885). I kept clearing my money beliefs (it becomes addictive when you see the results) and uncovering even more areas where I held myself back. Each time I broke through an income barrier, I uncovered even more negative self-beliefs and fears. One big fear was that it was a fluke. The first time I made over $10,000 in a month, I honestly felt sick and a little voice inside me said, *"no further, this is as far as you'll go"*.

I ignored it and kept decluttering and following the manifesting formula. Soon after, I had my first $10,000 week, then my first $10,000 day, now I've had several of those. I know I'll need to declutter more to make $10,000 in an hour. There's always more work to do. As David Neagle says, *"new level, new devil"* - each time you declutter you'll break through something you previously thought was impossible. If you're stuck, you just need to do more decluttering work and what I call "BE-cluttering" - decluttering your belief of what's possible.

This last month, I made ten times what I made at the same time last year. I've already done twice last year's revenue in the first five months of the year. (If all these numbers are stressing you out, that's okay, keep reading and you'll discover exactly why).

Guess what - I didn't get some fancy degree. I didn't get a lobotomy. I didn't suddenly become smarter. I didn't become a meth dealer. I didn't win the lottery.

I just decluttered my beliefs around money.

Are you getting how important this is?

It's tempting to subscribe to the lottery win fantasy or the complimentary upgrade fantasy, but there are quicker and more certain ways to manifest money than winning it. You have more chance of becoming a millionaire through your own ingenuity than through an arbitrary lottery win. You don't have to turn into an evil genius or do anything unethical.

"You and I are such similar creatures, Vivian.
We both screw people for money."
Edward Lewis in *Pretty Woman*

We all like to think that one day, we'll be at the back of the plane (having bought the cheapest ticket), and the stewardess comes up and says *"grab your bags, you're going to First Class!"*.

I know this *does* happen occasionally, but it's rare for the person on the plane who has invested the least to be upgraded. Generally, airlines reward people who have a *history of investing in* <u>*themselves*</u> first. That's why frequent fliers are the first to be upgraded.

Another way to look at it, is: *God helps those who help themselves.*

You know this is true in life and it's also been proved

in studies. Read *The Luck Factor*, by Richard Wiseman to see his studies of people who believe themselves to be lucky or unlucky. It's fascinating reading, as Wiseman confirms that luck is largely self-fulfilling.

"Happiness doesn't just flow from success;
it actually causes it."
Richard Wiseman

I remember one of the experiments in *The Luck Factor* vividly. The researchers placed a five dollar bill outside the research centre to see who noticed it and picked it up. Sure enough, the majority of the people who found it were the self-proclaimed lucky people. Why? Some people are convinced that lucky things happen to them all the time so they are constantly anticipating good news and opportunities, and some people are convinced that the world is against them so they are always waiting for the bad news. Which group would you rather be in?

According to Wiseman, here's how you can become more lucky:

1. **Maximise your chance opportunities.**
Build your network, have a relaxed attitude to life and be open to new experiences. (This is exactly how I manifested the free travel experience, I had a big network of people and just "happened" to hear about the competition).

2. **Listen to your lucky hunches.**
Take steps to develop your intuition and pay attention to your gut feelings. (For me, this is time away from my computer and putting myself in situations where I feel rich, that's when my intuition feels enhanced).

3. **Expect good fortune.**
Expect good things to happen to you, keep going in the face of failure, and tell yourself you're a lucky person. (When I'm in this frame of mind, it's amazing how many "lucky" things happen!)

4. **Turn your bad luck into good.**
See the positive side of bad luck, and don't dwell on bad situations (for me, this is becoming a "reverse paranoid" and assuming that *everything* that happens is ultimately for my highest good, even if it looks bad on the outside).

Oh crap, you're thinking, I'm not lucky at all!

First of all, if you *think* you're not lucky, the Universe will go out of its way to *prove* it to you. If you're always saying things like:

- *I'm so unlucky*
- *Typical, another bill!*
- *This* always *happens to me*
- *Why does the Universe hate me?*
- *Nothing good ever happens to me*
- *Why can't I be lucky too?*

I hate to tell you this, but YOU are creating it. Luck can be learned (obviously why you're reading this book), but it can take practice if you're used to being negative.

I'm not super positive all the time, but I'm pretty lucky. It's because I'm constantly saying things to myself and others like:

- *I'm so lucky!*
- *Thanks Universe for taking care of me*
- *Wow, another coin in the street, woo hoo!*

- *An unexpected bill, this must be a message from the Universe to pay attention*
- *Good things happen to me every day*
- *I'm so blessed and grateful*
- *This always happens to me!*
- *You'll never guess what I manifested today!*

See the difference? Lucky people are overwhelmingly grateful and take responsibility for their lives. The unlucky people are pessimistic and "hard done by". Even when something "bad" happens, I always look for the good, because my underlying story is "the Universe is always looking after my highest good".

Neil Patrick Harris agrees with me, "a lot of people would take getting rear-ended in their car as an example of why their life continues to be one road block after another, and I think a different person can see that same fender bender and be grateful it wasn't worse. That allows them an opportunity to learn something from it—sort of take some sort of positive elements from that. I think if you try to angle your life in those ways, then fate, destiny, karma opens itself up to you and allows for more growth".

I've had car accidents and that's exactly what I did, I thanked the Universe for the "wake up call" to pay more attention or get a safer car.

Manifesting outrageous abundance requires vigilance of your everyday thoughts about your ability to create luck and abundance. It means you have to be really careful about what you say to yourself and others about money.

At the beginning, it might feel forced, like you're just pretending to be happy - but that's okay! Pretending is like rehearsing and your brain can't tell the difference anyway.

"If you ask how they make decisions, 'lucky' people will talk about tuning in to information and instincts, while 'unlucky' people often mention pushing away the uncomfortable feeling they were headed for trouble."
Martha Beck, life coach

I remember when I first read the book *How to Win Friends and Influence People;* I think I was about 16 years old. The most important points I remember from that book were:

1. Eye contact
2. Giving compliments
3. Mirroring people

So, I started practicing. Even though it felt fake at first and I was consciously maintaining eye contact and trying to think of something to compliment, after a while, it became natural and just something I do.

Ditto with the positive thoughts. It's only when you become aware of your negative thoughts and feelings about money, will you be able to switch them around. It might feel like hard work at first because it's a deeply ingrained habit, but then it will become second nature.

The two examples I gave above about lucky and unlucky people were pretty obvious ones, so don't assume that you've decluttered everything about money and skip the next chapter. Your negative beliefs about your ability to be wealthier might be subtle but just as destructive. But that's where it starts to get fun! Imagine that you can easily break through your next income barrier just by re-examining your thoughts about money. You don't have to get smarter, you don't have to change gender, get a boob job, or grow three inches taller. You don't have to get skinnier before you deserve more money.

It's kind of ridiculous the "rules" we have about ourselves and *when* we can actually be rich. In this next chapter, we'll ruthlessly examine your current beliefs about what you're capable of and you'll learn amazing tools you can use to keep taking yourself through each income barrier.

Seriously, knowing and mastering this stuff will make you feel like you've got a superpower.

What if becoming rich was actually easy?

One of the very common fears for women of becoming rich is that you will have your nose to the grindstone 24 hours a day, seven days a week. That it will be such hard work that you probably shouldn't bother. That your kids will suffer if you got richer. Maybe you're already rapidly approaching burnout and thinking *"another 5, 10 years of this to get rich? I'll never make it"*.

I've had clients who just can't seem to slow down, because they feel like they should be working all the time and it's the only way to get rich. So paradoxically, they will never feel rich. They'll keep running, running, running and never get anywhere.

Movies and T.V. show us the burnt out exec who has a heart attack at 40 (remember the Friends episode where Phoebe was a stock-broker who has two heart attacks while yelling into her mobile?) or the "rich bitch" stereotype who lies and schemes to get what she wants at all costs.

"We don't pay taxes.
Only the little people pay taxes."
Leona Helmsley, The Queen of Mean

Who wants to be like that?!

I love movies so I did some digging around for more examples of the rich bitch. Look, I'm going a bit overboard here, but it's interesting to see what money messages go into our subconscious about what kind of women get rich. Play along.

Goldie Hawn in *Overboard,* was the rich bitch who yelled at her staff, *"I almost had to wait!"*, and only became nice when she lived a life of poverty with hunky Kurt Russell and his ragamuffin kids. Lesson - money makes you spoilt and bitchy, poverty makes you humble and nice.

What about *The Desperate Housewives* crew? Gabby was grasping and conniving, Bree was domineering and had serious OCD. The "nice" ones had the most financial problems and the messiest houses. Besides, the clue is in the name - they are mostly housewives married to rich guys. Lesson - you've got to marry to get rich.

Cher in *Clueless* was sweet, but dumb and spoiled and most of her rich friends were assholes. Regina George in *Mean Girls* was a conniving bitch who stomped over everyone else in school. Alexis in *Dallas,* the rich brats in *Gossip Girl,* Miranda Priestly in *Devil Wears Prada,* Cruella De Vil from *101 Dalmatians,* the women in *Revenge…* the list goes on. The lesson for all of us?

Rich = Bitch

Rich women in the music industry are divas, thought to have ridiculous commands (think J-Lo and Mariah Carey), to be aggressive perfectionists like Madonna or madcap eccentrics like Lady Gaga.

J-Lo apparently requires an all-white décor in her dressing rooms with lilies and Jo Malone candles, plus both refrigerated and room temp water. Of course, the papers use words like "diva demands" and "outrageous requests".

On *Basic Instinct 2*, Sharon Stone apparently requested Pilates equipment, a chauffeured car piloted by a non-smoking driver, two assistants, first-class travel and a deluxe motor home with air conditioning. Seriously though, how gross is it when you have to travel in a smoky car?!

This is probably completely fabricated bullshit but when Britney performed in London's O2 arena, she apparently requested platters of McDonald's cheeseburgers (no buns), 100 figs and prunes, and a framed photo of Princess Diana. Diva-licious!

Hell, I've even heard that the Queen of England requires a brand new toilet seat at every location while she's touring around the world. (So apparently does Mary J. Blige).

Regardless if any of this is true, what's the message to the average woman?

Rich = Diva

Despite the fact that these women have gotten to the point in their careers where they just want life to be easy, they have great boundaries in place to ensure consistent standards and they just ask for what they want, they are called "demanding".

My experience in travelling around the world and practically living in hotels is that it's annoying to try and do your job when you are surrounded by constant upheaval and change. If you hate feather pillows, are allergic to a certain type of flower or get sick with unfamiliar food, shouldn't you be able to ask for it without being called a diva?

Many businesses have a strict operating manual. Imagine if you were a McDonald's franchisee and you decided to go rogue? Nope.

So, if you're a performer and you're travelling around the world, why not have a strict operating manual so each show is just as high quality as the last? Of course, the men are seen as "rock'n'roll" and the women are just divas.

The papers are also full of stories about successful and wealthy women in the corporate world, but unfortunately they are shown to be aggressive, greedy, too busy to have children, too masculine or competitive. Politicians like Hilary Clinton, Margaret Thatcher, Julia Gillard and even Sarah Palin (not my favourite woman) are routinely told they are "shrill" and bitchy. They are often judged on their looks and clothing, not the message of their politics.

The movies show us that the only women in charge and successful are the hard-nosed, ice queen, money-obsessed, mean to the underlings, bitchy bosses like Miranda Priestly in *The Devil Wears Prada* yet again, Sandra Bullock's character in *The Proposal,* Demi Moore in *Disclosure,* Sigourney Weaver in *Working Girl* and Jennifer Aniston in *Horrible Bosses.* It was actually hard to find many more because so few women are depicted as leaders.

"Nice" bosses are usually broke but well-meaning women who run a sweet run down book shop or shabby chic bakery, like Meg Ryan in *You've Got Mail* or Kristen Wiig's character in *Bridesmaids.* The lesson that we're absorbing?

Rich = Ball-Breaker

So in a nutshell - rich women are demanding, spoilt, mean, bitchy to their friends, competitive, pretty on the outside but mean on the inside, demanding divas, conniving, materialistic, unethical, horrible to people they perceive as "underlings", lonely, much divorced, hen-peck their husbands, are shallow, superficial and kill puppies. They will lie, cheat, poison and steal to get what they want. They are gold-diggers, tax evaders, wicked step-mothers and evil Queens.

Can you think of many *nice* rich women from the movies? Usually only when they go out in the world and experience poverty, overcome a huge hardship or they are "rescued" and marry into their wealth with fucking Prince Charming.

"Don't marry for money. You can borrow it cheaper."
Lois P. Frankel

Movies aside, if any of this is ringing true for you, take some time to deconstruct your fears about becoming rich to find out where this is coming from. Even if you don't *think* you have any fears, play along, because trust me, there is *something* holding you back.

Jen had a fear that being successful meant total sacrifice. Her dad had a low paying job that he loved and it caused tension in the family because he had opportunities to get paid more but refused to because it would mean time away and longer hours. So, she did extremely well in her career but burnt herself out trying to prove she was living up to her potential, unlike her dad.

To her, success was either all or nothing, black or white. You can either love what you do but not reach the pinnacle of success materially, or you have a lot of money and a corporate job, but it's really stressful and a sacrifice to your family.

We think, *"If I am successful, I have to be ruthless and determined"*. Nope, you don't. You don't have to become Regina, Alexis, Cruella, Miranda or any other kind of rich bitch. You can still be YOU and be an awesome kind of rich woman. You just have to rewrite the script to suit your dreams for your life.

You can choose to be rich *and*:

Philanthropic
Gracious and friendly
A great role model for women
A leader and mentor
Inspiring to others
Generous to people around you
A creator of amazing experiences
A world explorer
An angel investor

You can create scholarships with your money. You can build the greenest, eco-technology-advanced house in the world. You can buy big chunks of the world's rainforest. You can explore the world. You can be an amazing role model for your kids, your family and your community. *You can change the world.*

"The easiest way for your children to learn about money is for you not to have any."
Katharine Whitehorn

You can choose to be like J.K Rowling who gave away so much of her money that she dropped down from the *Forbes* billionaire list to a mere multi-millionairess.

What about Oprah, who has created amazing things with her wealth, including her Angel Network which inspired giving all around the world and her school for young girls in South Africa. Nobody can dispute Oprah's legacy as one of the world's richest women.

Hey, it doesn't have to be all about *giving away* all your money. It's okay to keep it and use it for fun and pleasure too. It's totally okay to live the most outrageously luxurious life you want. We're told that it's "good" to be giving and "bad" to spend money on ourselves, but it's up to you how you'd like to spend your money.

You could fly around the world to see Adele in concert on your private jet. (You could probably hire Adele to sing on your private jet, just for you). You could have a private butler take care of your every whim in Zanzibar (I've experienced this, it's awesome). You could buy a $100,000 dress to go to the Oscars. Take off on a round-the-world cruise with other rich people. Buy an island. Meet up with your fellow lucky bitches to see Bette Midler in Vegas.

You might be thinking *"oh, but Denise, that's so*

ostentatious, so greedy, way too decadent".

The point is, gorgeous, that *nobody* can dictate to you what kind of rich person you are going to be. There are many shades of wealth. There are billionaires who dress like hobos, millionaires who drive twenty year old cars, middle class people who go on spectacular holidays, average people who have cleaners and private chefs, paupers who live like kings on credit cards and everything in between. *There's no rule that you have to be a rich bitch.* Only you decide.

"I'd like to live like a poor man with lots of money."
Pablo Picasso

For awesome rich girl inspiration, check out Beyoncé's official Tumblr page. You'll see photos from her daily life in all its luxurious glory. Girlfriend is enjoying her wealth and she was plenty rich enough before marrying JayZ. I also love reading Gwyneth Paltrow's blog, GOOP. Google her travel tips and you'll get an insight into how a wealthy and stylish woman travels. Again, she's made her own money and still seems like a nice person. I even love reading the Rich Kids on Tumblr blog because even though it's so crazy and ostentatious, I love to see what emotions it brings up for me, so I can clear it. I don't aspire to be a rich asshole, but it's not a good emotion to hate them or begrudge their wealth either.

Role model other amazing wealthy women like Ellen DeGeneres, Sara Blakely (the creator of Spanx), Martha Stewart, Sheryl Sandberg, Diane Von Furstenberg, Anna Wintour, Tyra Banks or Gisele Bundchen. Read their autobiographies or if you get the chance, see them speak.

Find amazing philanthropists to model by reading Forbes' annual rich lists.

Your financial role model might be your grandma or your local lady politician. They don't have to be a billionaire or a business woman, it could be someone that you really admire for their values and grace in the public eye like Michelle Obama or Julia Gillard. Basically, follow in rich women's footsteps and you'll feel good about being rich too.

> *"I wanna be a billionaire so frickin bad Buy all of the things I never had I wanna be on the cover of Forbes Magazine Smiling next to Oprah and the Queen."*
> Travis McCoy (Ft. Bruno Mars), *Billionaire*

Turn your attention to great stories of wealthy women (and men) and ignore the negative ones about the guilt of working mothers, lengthy court battles over wealth, nasty divorces and rich women acting just as greedy as the greediest man. Most of that stuff is a distraction and can make you feel fearful about wealth. Engaging in debates designed to fuel the "mommy wars" is just as destructive. Ignore it all.

Inspire yourself by reading books about successful women, and you'll see how they overcame their own struggles with negative people, how they build up their self-confidence and how they made and spend their money.

Chapter Summary

- Choose your money role models carefully, and ignore the bad ones.
- Watch your money thoughts constantly. You have to be vigilant.
- You can release the stereotypes of what rich women are in the world and create your own meaning of wealth. Bonus - get my top 10 list of must-read money books for women.
  Get it at www.GetRichLuckyBitch.com

$

Clear Your Past Money Dramas

"Taking responsibility for your beliefs and judgments gives you the power to change them."
Byron Katie

We've all got our own money dramas and maybe some of the celebrity money stories hit a little too close to home. Have you identified your major money sabotages yet?

Are you:

- *Overgenerous*
- *Overspending to impress other people*
- *Spending on drugs, alcohol or shopping to make yourself feel good*
- *Spending out of guilt or obligation*
- *Saving other people from their financial dramas or problems*
- *Giving away your power to other people in your life?*

If you've identified a few areas where you're sabotaging yourself, fantastic! The more self-aware you can be about your money behaviours, the better and the quicker you'll move to the next income level. Think of it like a game of *Snakes & Ladders* – when you engage in self-sabotaging behaviour you slide down the snake and go backwards. When you acknowledge and clear those beliefs, you get to climb the ladder and make fast progress.

Like most things in our lives, the way we handle money has a lot to do with our past experiences and what we've seen or learned while growing up.

When I work with my clients 1:1 and with my *Lucky Bitch Money Bootcamp* participants, we spend more than 80% of our time on decluttering old beliefs, cleaning up bad money habits and my favourite personal development technique – forgiveness. I bang on about forgiveness all day long, for one simple reason – it works miracles in all areas of our life and allows the money to flow naturally. It's just the shit you have to wade through before things can be easy.

Imagine that you have your own personal river of abundance that can never run dry. It can flow to you all day and night with everything you need to live an amazing life. However, only a trickle of your true abundance can ever get to you. That's because you've got blocks in the way – maybe massive boulders that represent your negative beliefs around money and each negative money memory blocks it up even more. If you're at the bottom of the river, you can only see what's coming to you, a tiny trickle. It represents such a small amount of what's available to you, and the only way to remove those self-imposed barriers is to identify and destroy them forever. Luckily forgiveness dissolves even the biggest obstacles.

You might've had a childhood where money was really tight and you've got funny but kind of sad stories about your cheap-ass dad or the Christmas where you got the most awful present ever, so that's why you overspend for your own friends and family, in an effort to exorcise those yucky and embarrassing memories.

Or, maybe you had rich parents who spent money like crazy to the point of embarrassment, or maybe you had a rich uncle who paid for everything, or a friend who was really poor and made you feel guilty for having money, so you unconsciously push it away as an adult by making bad financial decisions in an effort not to be the "rich bitch".

These experiences have shaped who you are today and they might be holding you back from becoming your best and wealthiest self now and in the future. When we do radical emotional de-cluttering on past money experiences you can start with a new fresh perspective on money and allow your natural abundance to flow.

Emotional clearing through forgiveness is a non-negotiable process if you want to be rich, and even if you've done it before, try it again with a specific money focus because there's *always* more to uncover. In the world of manifesting, negative emotion is really the only thing that holds us back.

Release Old Money Drama

If you want to earn more money, you must release *any* negative energy you have around money no matter how small.

You have to be willing to look at any memories from your past that have any attachment to money, especially events where you felt angry, sad, embarrassed, or humiliated. Find any memory of old arguments or resentments over money or anything that explains why you act the way you do now with your money.

The first time I did this exercise, I wrote five pages worth of stuff that I still felt angry about, like bosses from years back who didn't give me a pay increase (those bastards!), anger towards a family member for a cheap, skanky birthday present, or my step-dad and his strict rules around pocket money.

Some of that shit was *years old* and I was still thinking about it. You bet that forgiving and clearing all that old money drama gave me permission to rapidly increase my income. The only reason I could even make that first $225 is because I started decluttering my money memories. But I didn't want to get stuck at that income level, so I kept going and kept forgiving.

And you know what? When I tried to replicate that original list a couple of months later to see if there was anything left, most of it was gone. I had let it go, I was over it, I was free of it. Forever.

Holding on to the energy of money drama is incredibly subtle. You might not think you even *have* any money drama left from your life. Well, you'd be surprised. Most people have at least a few major incidences around money that are affecting them as adult women today.

Go through your life chronologically. Start from your earliest memory about money and work your way up.

What do you remember about money?

For example, you might've felt angry when someone stole money from you in the sixth grade. It embarrassed and humiliated you. That feeling of shame and helplessness still lives within you today.

Or you could have stolen money from someone else and the memory of it makes you squirm, because you are still carrying the shame and guilt of the "thief" tag. You might not think about it every day, but trust me, it's still there.

Maybe you felt poor when you had to wear an old suit to a job interview. You remember vividly how it felt to hold yourself so a stain or rip wouldn't show. It made you feel inferior to all the well-dressed people around you. That version of yourself still lives inside you sometimes and that leftover whiff of inferiority holds you back from being rich.

Maybe you were embarrassed for a friend because she was short of cash at University and it was excruciating every time the restaurant bill came. Your compassion and empathy for her actually caused you to feel her emotions for her and *that* is still living inside you.

Embarrassment is such a powerful emotion around money. You could be embarrassed that you're rich, embarrassed that you're poor. It doesn't always have to be about being broke - you could be embarrassed that your parents were wealthy.

"Money, if it does not bring you happiness, will at least help you be miserable in comfort."
Helen Gurley Brown

Think about your career. Were you ever unfairly denied a pay rise and it still hurts when you think of the *injustice* of it? Maybe you found out that you were paid less than a co-worker and it seriously pissed you off but you couldn't say anything. I would lay awake at night rehashing old conversations with my pig of a boss and get *so* angry. It's not good for your blood pressure and not good for manifesting money!

What about your relationships. Remember any money situations that relate to your boyfriend, girlfriend, partner, or ex-partners. You should get some juicy memories around them and trust me, they are *still* living with you.

One thing that came up for me was a memory about a boyfriend that I had at university. He was a real tight-arse. He would order all this expensive food and then he would be really cheap when it came to the bill. We went out to dinner with my mum and he said *"Vicki, you had the prawns so you should pay more"*. So he went on my money clearing list. It might be a small memory but I never want to take any chances. If you still remember it with *any* kind of emotion, it's something you should clear. Remember – throw *everything* at it. It's the equivalent of practicing your scales to master the piano.

You can go on adding to your money forgiveness list as much as you want. Anyone and anything related to money that still gives you an emotional charge should go on your list. It doesn't matter how small or large the memory, we're doing a deep clean and leaving nothing to chance.

Creating the list could take you anything from 10 minutes to hours and hours. As you go through this book I encourage you to always add things to your forgiveness list. It's not something we do once and then just forget about it. I still add situations and memories to my list.

Now... forgive and set yourself free

Ok, so you have your list. The hard part is almost over, because most people procrastinate actually doing the list in the first place, so I applaud your bravery and commitment. No need to burn the list or do any weird Voodoo rituals, you just clear it through energetic forgiveness.

Here's what you do: go through each item one at a time. Take time to think about that incident and what it meant to you. Let any residual emotion come up and then you say, "I forgive you. I'm sorry. And I love you." It's so simple. Don't think because it's simple it's not going to work. It's incredibly powerful stuff and is based on Ho'oponopono, the gentle Hawaiian practice of reconciliation and forgiveness. It will change your life for the better.

Photographer from Adelaide, Emma Pointon shared this in my Bootcamp, *"I started my forgiveness exercise this morning... it made me feel physically sick while doing it but after I felt lighter. I think that the process will have to be rinse and repeat, rinse and repeat. Lots to clear, lots to forgive, lots to release to the Universe"*.

Some people definitely have that reaction, but it's worth it to continue.

Why Forgiveness Works

Let me explain each part of the forgiveness mantra. The forgiving part is really to release you from the energy of the memory.

"I'm sorry" is acknowledging that, maybe at some soul level, you played a little part in that happening. Maybe

you were a vibrational match for that situation to happen to you, because of a higher lesson. It could have been a contract that your soul agreed to. That can be hard to hear but I say just go with it and do it, anyway. You don't have to mean it 100% for it to be effective. Really I mean that. You don't have to mean it fully. Just try it.

We finish the mantra with, *"I love you,"* because love is the most powerful force in the Universe. Love can transform anything. It doesn't mean that you necessarily love that person; it doesn't mean you have to call them to say that you love them; it's just an intention and a blessing from a soul to soul level. It doesn't mean you condone what they did to you. It doesn't mean that you forget. You just release it from your own energetic field.

> *"When you plant lettuce, if it does not grow well, you don't blame the lettuce. You look into the reasons it is not doing well. It may need fertilizer, or more water, or less sun. You never blame the lettuce. Yet if we have problems with our friends or our family, we blame the other person. But if we know how to take care of them, they will grow well, like lettuce. Blaming has no positive effect at all, nor does trying to persuade using reason and arguments. That is my experience. No blame, no reasoning, no argument, just understanding. If you understand, and you show that you understand, you can love, and the situation will change."*
>
> Thích Nhat Hanh

If you skip one of the forgiveness mantras, it's going to be unbalanced and it's more about blame than acceptance and forgiveness. Blame just means that you're still carrying the memory. The Universe loves harmony and balance and so does money.

You might think, *"I'm not going to forgive that asshole, Denise. Are you serious?!"*

Ok sweets - your choice. All I can do is share with you the complete transformation I've made in my life purely through the power of forgiveness. Forgiveness has nothing to do with the other person and all about giving yourself permission to be worthy of love and forgiveness yourself.

Money Mantra:
The more I forgive, the more money I earn because I allow myself to receive.

Make forgiveness a regular part of your life. Parisa Eithne Roohipour, a yoga teacher in Vancouver told me, *"Sometimes I do forgiveness in the shower so I feel like the ickyness is being washed down the plug hole"*.

Just like brushing your teeth and washing your hair, forgiveness can make you feel squeaky clean every day and *worthy* every day. When you feel worthy, you can attract money easily.

Keep going over your forgiveness list until it has no emotional charge anymore. Some things will be gone. You'll forget them forever. It'll just be lifted out of your heart and lifted out of your soul to make room for other, lighter emotions. Some memories will stay with you and take longer to shift.

I told you I was going to be straight with you. Here's the honest truth - you'll probably have to do the forgiveness process again and again, probably til you die. It doesn't mean you spend your whole life doing it. It just means that every time you hit a new money block, go back to forgiveness – it's that powerful.

Be more persistent than your ego, because it wants to believe that you are right in being pissed off. Your ego wants to hold the grudge, but do you want to be right or *rich*?

Are you ready to let go and forgive?

How Forgiveness Shifted Her Self-worth

One client loved doing this forgiveness work because she experienced such a profound transformation of her current reality and in turn, her own self-worth.

Kristy discovered that she held some hidden resentment and anger towards her husband which completely "validated" her feeling that she wasn't being cherished or valued. She uncovered a small but symbolic memory: when her husband proposed he didn't have a proper engagement ring, instead giving her a silver ring with a blue stone which in Kristy's words, "looked like a piece of glass". Of course, everyone wanted to see her engagement ring but she was so embarrassed, and to make things even worse, after a week, it started turning her hand green. For her, the whole experience was humiliating. At a time when you are meant to be feeling full of love and excitement and proud to be engaged, Kristy was feeling embarrassed. That experience set her up for a lifetime of feeling neglected by her husband (even when it wasn't true). It's sad how we make stories up about ourselves, instead of letting go. Her story became "I don't matter".

"I didn't even realise until many years later that this was such a pattern in my relationship with my husband. It never occurred to him to maybe get a job for a month or two and save up some money and actually give me a ring when he proposed.

"It also never occurred to me that what I really wanted was for a man to say, 'You are so important to me. I love you so much. You're so exquisite. You are the woman I want to wake up with for the rest of my life and I value you so much that I want to give you something that reflects just a speck of your beauty'," Kristy said.

"Later, I realised I've always held back my respect, love and adoration for him as a man, because I think, well, you can't really take care of me," Kristy said.

This pattern repeated itself throughout Kristy's marriage and consequently made her feel that she was unworthy and undeserving of nice things. She let that story become part of who she was to the extent she felt like she had to always prove herself and work really hard to do things on her own.

So of course, that story leaked into her own sense of value and when we looked at Kristy actually earning more, clearing this story became incredibly important. Can you see the (now obvious) connection?

"My journey in the last year has really been about entitling myself to have exactly what it is that lights me up without having to justify it, without having to work for it so hard. My story has always been that I work so hard and exhaust myself in the process of trying to prove that I'm worthy of something," Kristy said.

By saying "I forgive you, I'm sorry, and I love you", Kristy was really saying "I forgive you" to herself. She was forgiving herself for believing that she was undeserving. It helped her realise that she had been holding her husband in contempt for the ways he had wronged her.

"For me, what I was doing was synonymous with shutting off life. That flow of life had not been available to me in the ways that I really wanted, and I know it was directly related to holding him in contempt and maintaining that level of pain over those old memories for so long," Kristy said.

By working through this forgiveness exercise Kristy was able move past the contempt, forgive herself and her husband and move on to freedom.

Forgiveness is the gift that you give yourself. Who are the people in your life that you are holding in contempt? What past wrongs are you holding on to?

Who are you ready to forgive?

Forgiveness is one of those things that people always try and skip, because it just seems like either too much hard work or a little bit unnecessary.

I haven't had kids, but forgiveness is like what my mum was telling me about childbirth - you can't bargain your way out of it. She had me, her first born and then she forgot about the pain. Then when she was having my brother, she remembered how painful it was and she was trying to bargain her way out of it and was saying to the midwives, "no, no, I don't want to have a baby today, I think I've changed my mind". And the midwives said, "sorry lady, you can't bargain your way out of this one, it's happening whether you like it or not".

Forgiveness is usually scarier before you do it but the end result is so worthwhile because without it you can't move forward. But it's completely normal to think, *"No, it's going to hurt! It's going to be messy and ugly. I don't want to do it, don't make me, Denise!"*

So while it might be painful to do this exercise, and there might be some tears, it really is worth doing (seriously, I can't emphasise this enough). As well as strengthening your manifesting muscle, forgiveness and emotional clearing will leave you lighter and happier and open your river of abundance even more.

Clean house... literally

While this isn't a Feng Shui book, a great complementary exercise when you're decluttering your emotions is to physically declutter your home of crap, clutter, or anything that reminds you of negative past experiences. Throw out old unwanted gifts or give them to charity, get rid of old items you don't really like, make room for the new things that you can buy with the money that will be coming to you. If you really treasure an item but still want to get rid of it, take a photo of it then give it away. You'll feel lighter and you'll make space for more.

Giving Up the Guilt

At various stages throughout your energetic journey to more money you might come across one of the most common feelings women suffer - guilt.

You might feel guilty for wanting more, or for spending money on yourself, or for taking time out of your busy family life to work on improving yourself. You might feel guilty that other people are poor, that your friend is jealous, that there are starving people in the world. Many women on my money Bootcamp start to feel guilty that it's suddenly really easy to make money. I've definitely had the guilts when I increased my prices to well beyond what my colleagues were charging or more than my friends or family earned.

Women - we are guilt-ridden creatures. But the answer to this lies in the forgiveness work.

No one can make you feel guilty without your consent.

One of the common questions I'm asked is how do I stop feeling guilty when I'm in debt? I don't deserve to spend money.

I think this guilt is such a female thing. Many male successful entrepreneurs (think Donald Trump and Richard Branson) have gone to the brink financially many times, gambling on their business success with credit card debt and huge bank loans, and then let their various businesses go bankrupt if they weren't successful. These guys have their past littered with the carcasses of forgotten or failed business ventures. *"That's business,"* you'll hear these type of men say; *"it's not personal"*.

Well, for women it IS personal and I bet that you've got some failures from your past that you're ashamed of. Most women would rather die of shame than go bankrupt and not pay their suppliers. Most women see past business failure less about the valuable business experience and more as a personal failure. You think, *"I'm obviously not good at business"*.

"What we perceive as a failure may simply be our inner being's way of telling us that we are ready to move to a new level of growth."
Anne Wilson Schaef

Forgive yourself for past business failures. You tried your best and it was only a practice for the next thing. It's a journey.

So, in the spirit of "come at it from all angles", I listed every single business failure, from the embarrassing (having a dismal multi-level marketing business) to the ill-conceived (my Raw Brides business) and even my little business ventures as a kid. I figured that if any of those failures still followed me around in any way, it wouldn't hurt to release them in order to make way to new and profitable business ideas.

Take it one step further. Forgive your business partners and forgive the companies, suppliers, customers and agencies you worked with. While you're at it – forgive the taxation department, bankers, the Government, the economy and the President or Prime Minister. You might think that's going overboard, but it can't hurt, right?

"Letting go gives us freedom, and freedom is the only condition for happiness."
Thich Nhat Hanh

The beautiful thing with doing this multi-layered work around forgiveness is that it eliminates these feelings of guilt and unworthiness in your future businesses that could repel customers and opportunities. When you forgive yourself and others, it gives you permission to do more, have more, be more in your life without sabotaging it all through guilt or unworthiness.

Even if you've failed in the past, you now give yourself permission to earn money easily.

I remember really early on in my relationship with Mark, I had this big guilt trip about buying new clothes. I used to only shop at second-hand stores, and there's nothing wrong with that, but it was how it made me *feel* that wasn't in alignment to wealth. I didn't believe that I deserved to have the exact size, colour, shape and perfect fit that you can only find when buying brand new clothes. I believed deep down that I deserved only to have cast-offs and that I had to settle for what other people had thrown away.

I remember walking the street with Mark past a shop window and he would say, *"Oh don't even look"*, because we were so broke. He would put his hand over my eyes and literally *drag* me away from the store window. I let that happen because he was just mirroring my thoughts about myself, which were, *"You don't even deserve to go in the store and try on the clothes, let alone even look. You are not worth it"*.

He had his own issues around money at that time as well, so we worked on this together. I said to him, *"Buddy, what are you doing? I'm just looking. You're making me feel shit about money. You are keeping me in this headspace just as much as I am; you're being complicit in this"*.

Of course, I forgave him and myself and looked at memories of my childhood to clear where I *didn't* feel worthy of brand new clothes, or guilty when I asked my mum to buy me something she couldn't afford.

Step by step, I let myself go into the store, and gave

myself permission to try on some new clothes. I then started to buy things, but it was a gradual process. It took me years to stop shopping in second-hand stores, as I cleared and forgave old memories and beliefs. I was in one recently and while looking around I noticed I started to feel uncomfortable and wasn't really enjoying being in there because all those feelings of unworthiness were coming back. I just wanted to go into a store where I could say, "This is my size; I want it in red, black, blue", and then just buy it if I liked it.

I recently stepped it up a notch and bought an expensive dress a little out of my comfort zone and in an area of the department store that I would automatically avoid as being "too expensive". I seriously walk my talk girlfriend, and there's always more to uncover, I'm always trying to increase my capacity for wealth, a tiny bit at a time.

As I was trying on all of these expensive dresses, I noticed how nice the material felt and saw that the fit really was different. Not only that, I bought a new clutch and wore brand new shoes. I wore it that weekend at a wedding with my hair professionally blow-dried. I felt amazing. But I had to stop myself automatically going to the sale rack and allow myself to try on clothes based on what I *liked*, rather than what I thought I could afford. You know, when you look at the price tag before you really look at the dress to see if you like it?

I never suggest living beyond your means and putting material doodads on your credit card to keep up with your stylish or rich friend. You have to start where you are and just upgrade incrementally to the next step. If you always shop at Target, you're not going to buy your next outfit at

Prada. It will feel energetically wrong and you'll find a way to sabotage it somehow. Just choose the next step up. That way you won't freak out your ego. It takes time to truly and permanently increase your standards.

That's not to say there is something wrong with buying second-hand clothes or shopping at Target. It's all about how it makes you *feel*. If you love the thrill of seeking out and finding hidden treasures in vintage shops and second-hand stores then keep doing it! If it makes you feel great to wear beautiful vintage clothes then go ahead. For me it wasn't about wearing the clothes, it was about how it made me *feel* - like I wasn't worth spending the extra money on buying new clothes. But if you love it, by all means continue doing it.

"I like my money where I can see it,
hanging in my closet."
Carrie Bradshaw in *Sex and the City*

It sucks but it's true that women feel guilty more often than than men. You rarely hear a man say, *"I feel so guilty, I just had a piece of cake."* We feel guilty about wanting things for ourselves instead of being in sacrifice to someone else. We feel guilty about wanting big dreams for our life. We feel guilty about earning fabulous money.

I definitely felt guilty when I started my business because it started being really easy to make money doing what I love. I work at home in my yoga clothes, and sometimes even in my pyjamas. It's just this really chilled and relaxed lifestyle. Sometimes I work really long hours, and sometimes I'll just go off and see a movie. People have said to me *"Oh you're so naughty"*, and I try to ignore that initial feeling of guilt and make myself say, *"No, this is how I've designed my life"*. I'm self-employed because that is how I want to live my life. I want to be able to go to the movies on a Tuesday afternoon if I want. Part of that has been giving up the guilt of other people's opinions about what I should and shouldn't do.

"Money is the best deodorant."
Elizabeth Taylor

My friend and mastermind buddy Leonie Dawson works just a few hours a day on her business and she turns over at least half a million dollars (and counting). When she gave up the expectation of what other people thought she should do, her business thrived.

She taught me her secret mantra... are you ready? It's "Fuckem". Her philosophy is to be happy and if other people criticise you for that, it's their problem.

Along with forgiving past business failures, forgive yourself for how you've handled money in the past - whether it's from getting into debt or wasting money on a bad investment.

When I was twenty, I discovered this amazing thing called "Interest Free Credit". I literally had no idea how this worked (hmmm, do you see the need for basic financial literacy in schools?). All I knew is that my friend Mazzy went into this electronic store and answered a few questions and walked out with a brand new laptop. Awesomeness! So, me and three friends went to get ourselves some of this action. There is no way I should have been approved, so when the salesman was filling out my application, he said "let's just say that your boyfriend pays your rent". I was like "sweet!". Twenty minutes later, I walked out with a brand new laptop... that I couldn't afford.

Well – you know how it goes. Once the interest free part finishes, you end up paying a ridiculous amount of interest. I moved overseas and failed to make payments, giving myself a terrible credit score. My mum had to pay off that loan and the worst part is that the laptop got stolen.

I could tell you many other stupid stories around money and debt, but I'm sure you have a few of your own, right?

These experiences give us a framework to how we view our capacity to earn and keep money. By constantly doing forgiveness work on those memories and by examining your past experiences in handling money, those feelings of unworthiness can be cleared and you'll give yourself permission to earn more.

Release Family Money Drama

For some people the forgiveness work can be a long process and a very intense time that opens up your eyes to the deep underlying issues you have around money. It could start to feel insurmountable, so just do one forgiveness mantra at a time. It's only going to be ugly for a short time as you're cleaning out all the crap. It will never be as intense as the first time you do it.

For one of my Bootcamp ladies, Victoria, the intensity of the forgiveness work surprised her. She came from a comfortable middle-class background, but when her family's business failed, the family was forced to follow her father across the country in pursuit of money. So from an early age she learnt that money stresses people out. Her mum would tell her *"don't tell your father"*, when she spent money or would encourage her to lie about prices. Who shares that memory too?!

She got married to a man who had his own issues with money. Her husband always said he never wanted to feel like he didn't have enough money, because those times were so traumatic for him as a kid. So she kept all the finance matters hidden from him so he would never know when they were down to their last cent. Instead she carried the burden of their financial pressures solely on her shoulders. She was stressed and her husband was blissfully unaware, which of course meant that she resented him for it.

By doing the forgiveness work, Victoria realised it was not her husband's fault that she kept everything from him, it's what she had seen her own mother do. She was really forgiving herself *and* her mother for the past.

After doing the forgiveness work, another client Natasha said: "It just felt really good. Also, it reminded me that I'm human and that it's okay not to be perfect. What this exercise has shown me that maybe I'm not so good with money, but there are a 150 things that my mum told me when I was growing up that have led to me having this particular attitude towards money. As long as I can identify those things and understand where they come from, then I can start working through them and letting them go".

It's not even your parent's fault. They learned their money beliefs from their parents and so on. Your mother learnt to lie about prices from *her* mother and you can break the cycle.

When Francesca was young her father passed away and her step-dad's behaviour caused her mother to go bankrupt.

Francesca was switched on to the fact that this negative emotional experience could impact on her own marriage and the way she dealt with her own money as an adult. Francesca did some forgiveness work around this experience in an effort to move away from the fear that her own husband would cause her financial and emotional distress.

"I have done a lot of healing around this and now feel comfortable with having nice things and not worrying about the money too much except for being responsible and paying my bills," Francesca said. However, some aspects of that experience still linger in her mind:

"My husband doesn't know that I have this secret savings account with money in it. I've always had this fear that I would end up making a lot of money and I would end up with a dodgy husband like my step-dad who would take all of it," Francesca said.

Although Francesca was part way there with her healing around this experience, she had to go one step further and forgive herself for her present actions so she could have a healthy, adult relationship with her husband and their finances.

Hiding money from your partner through fear brings up some uncomfortable truths you might need to face. What are you afraid of? Why is this behaviour happening, is it something you saw your own parents do?

Clear it so it doesn't become your reality.

My Favourite Self-Belief Clearing Tool

One of the best tools I know to eliminate negative beliefs is Emotional Freedom Technique (EFT). It's totally awesome, free and more importantly, it works.

Based on the principles of acupressure, EFT is a simple tapping exercise that removes negative fears and self-beliefs. It's not invasive at all and it's something that you can do to yourself.

EFT centres on the theory that negative emotional experiences disturb the energy meridians that run through our body. By using your fingertips to tap on key points on your face and body while focusing on a problem or negative feeling, EFT quickly realigns the energy meridians associated with those memories, allowing healing to occur. It's a great tool to effectively calm or soothe yourself emotionally, mentally and physically. It sounds strange but it's really easy and effective. (Remember, it all works, throw everything at it!)

I've used it in so many ways in my life and I still use it today. I've used it to eliminate decade-long habits and when I feel fear or anxiety. EFT can be done anywhere if you do it discreetly. I always do it before I speak on stage or you can nip into the bathroom before a scary interview. I even do it at the traffic lights when I'm driving.

While you are tapping on the key points around your face and body, you say the mantra:

"Even though I have this fear, I deeply and completely love and accept myself."

The mantra is the most important part. By tapping on the various points and by saying to yourself, even if the very worst thing about you was true, you deeply and completely love and accept yourself anyway. You can get even more specific so instead of saying something generic like "this fear", you start to name out loud what you're most scared about.

It could be...

- *Even though I have this debt...*
- *Even though I'm terrible with money...*
- *Even though I brought this on myself...*
- *Even though I don't deserve to be rich...*

Get real, raw and very specific and always finish with... *I deeply and completely love and accept myself.*

That self-acceptance at a soul level is incredibly powerful, because it releases you to take action, because then you know it's never going to be as bad as you think. It's just reassurance to yourself at a soul level, that everything is ok. You are safe and you are loved. It's similar to the radical self-love work that Louise Hay teaches. From a manifesting point of view, it also allows you to receive because you believe at a cellular level that you deserve it no matter what.

Accepting yourself at soul level releases you to take action and receive.

You can use EFT every single day just to clear some of the old crappy emotions that reveal themselves as you earn more money. I love EFT and I use it all the time, especially when I'm in a scary situation, like if I'm about to go on stage or have an important conversation with someone. It is going to make a crazy amount of difference in your manifestation and dealing with all those pesky negative feelings that come up.

With EFT you become responsible for soothing or

calming yourself, instead of waiting for another person to change your mood, attitude or behaviour so you can feel better immediately, and we know that good feelings attract good things. You can find tonnes of EFT videos on YouTube and I recommend doing it as a daily success habit.

"Because one believes in oneself, one doesn't try to convince others. Because one is content with oneself, one doesn't need others' approval. Because one accepts oneself, the whole world accepts him or her."
Lao Tzu

When Forgiveness Isn't Enough

If something's not working for you at the moment in your life, whether it's with money or anything else, remember my philosophy - throw *everything* at it. Something WILL work but it's the intention behind the action that matters more than the particular technique.

I'm going to just share with you a few things that have really helped me and the clients I work with to clear negativity.

I see a kinesiologist / energy healer at least once a month. A kinesiologist is somebody who works with the energy in your body. They do muscle testing to see where you've got blockages such as hormonal, energetic, or physical problems, and in particular, help you clear toxic emotions that you're holding onto.

I discovered kinesiology a couple of years ago when I was deep in my healing journey (when I was also broke but I wasn't ready to work on my money stuff). I also send all of my clients to kinesiologists. Combined with goal coaching, it's an unbeatable combination for rapid success.

Anyway, I was really, really unhappy and I was starting to declutter things in my life; old friends, unhealthy work situations and even addictive junk food. In the midst of all this emotional upheaval (and Saturn Return), my grandmother died. A few months later, I was in hospital with pneumonia. Everything was going wrong.

A friend saw the emotional state I was in and recommended kinesiology. And I immediately thought, *"I can't afford that"*. It was about £90.00 and it seemed like a lot of money just to talk to someone in an unknown (to me) method, and at that time I was very, very stingy with myself. But I decided to scrape up the money somehow, and it turned into such an unbelievable experience and healing for me that led me to change even MORE things about my life. Everything works and you are worth spending money on.

Remember, there's no such thing as an overnight success. My healing journey took many years to get to the point where I allowed myself to have even basic comforts, let alone give myself permission to be rich. If you feel like you're stuck, you've got to deal with the basic stuff before you can move on to the money.

In my session with the kinesiologist, Francoise, she asked me about my pneumonia, *"Has someone in your family died recently?"*. I just burst into tears. Then she told me, *"our lungs are where we hold onto grief in our life, and that's why you've created your sickness in that area"*. I was just blown away by it.

I had to declutter at a really physical base level, so I suggest that if you're feeling really stuck, or just want to take your well-being to a completely new level, make an appointment to see a kinesiologist.

Emotions live in our bodies. Old experiences, thoughts and feelings can impact our current reality. As we know from Louise Hay, illness can be manifested in our bodies. It can be really tough to push through on will power alone or to be stoic about it, *"I* will not *let this affect me"*. Sometimes that's completely out of your control, and it's not your fault. The great news as always, is that if you clear it, it can release the energy to work on something else.

One of my private coaching clients wasn't making progress in her goals. She was so stuck in her negative self-beliefs and it was frustrating for both of us. When I probed into significant events from her past, she told me she had a car accident five years earlier. She had hit somebody and although thankfully they didn't die, it made her very nervous to drive because every time she got in the car, she remembered it. Although she didn't say so directly, that significant event created a story of *"I'm a bad person. I don't deserve to be happy"*. So, I sent her to a kinesiologist so she could release it and avoid repeating her biggest fear (hitting someone again) or have that emotion show up in a different way of self-sabotage.

You can't create an amazing life and receive outrageous abundance with an underlying fear that you're a bad person. You can't be a vibrational match to happiness and wealth while holding on to unnecessary fear, and without a doubt you'll find a way to sabotage any success you manage to get through will-power alone.

Another client had a really traumatic experience a few years before when she was carjacked and robbed at gun-point and told she was going to be killed. That significant traumatic event splintered her world, despite trying her best to get over it.

Although she didn't think about it every day, she made an unconscious decision on that day that the world was not a safe place. Although she made great money in her business, she became very overweight after that scary day. The weight became her protection from the world. So I said to her, *"Look, life coaching is great, but find out where that event lives in your body, and just get rid of it"*. She had therapy and had mentally recovered from the experience but she needed to go one step further to an energetic level, so she saw a kinesiologist and immediately felt better. I haven't spoken to her in a few years, but I bet that her income has increased and her weight has gone in the other direction.

My grandmother had recovered from breast cancer, and then she died of a brain tumour. She was a lovely, beautiful woman, and I loved her very, very much, but she held onto this resentment of my granddad for years and a lot of suppressed anger. Did she create her illness? I'm not a doctor, clearly, but I believe that we can manifest things in our life negatively if we hold onto emotions of anger, resentment and fear. At the very least, it would create conditions in our body (anxiety, stress, elevated blood pressure, depression) conducive to illness, especially cancer.

My years of being spectacularly unsuccessful in my business and career was directly aligned to my underlying feeling there was something wrong with me. I was "bad" somehow. I had a lot of "evidence" to prove it - old memories and circumstances that I really had no control over. Clearing everything, allowed me to change my story, that I was worthy of abundance, just like anyone else.

The bad memories and self-blame will show up in many ways - sabotaging yourself or in chronic bad health. Not coincidentally, I had many examples of bad health in my twenties. True abundance is completely aligned to good health and when one suffers, the other usually does too.

"Money cannot buy health, but I'd settle for a diamond studded wheelchair."
Dorothy Parker

How To Love Yourself At A Cellular Level

It doesn't have to be kinesiology, you can try many different treatments. I've done acupuncture, energy work, Access Consciousness, Byron Katie's The Work, The Journey, meditation, Landmark Education, yoga - it all works so try to see what resonates with you and your belief system. There's nothing out there that's "better" than anything else. Try something and see.

As long as the message behind the methodology comes back to self-love and acceptance, you'll heal yourself from the past.

I was talking to a friend today who had breast cancer in her early 30s and she said the exact same thing. You really have to love yourself at a cellular level to come back from that sort of devastating illness. She recently had her blood tested and she could literally see her cells, all healthy after she put her cancer behind her. She combined traditional treatment with meditation and deliberately cultivating loving kindness in her life to love herself at a cellular level. It didn't cure her cancer, but I'm sure it contributed to her recovery.

Dr. Masaru Emoto's famous book, *The Hidden Messages in Water* is a fascinating example of this. He did experiments on vials of water, by putting messages on them and thinking deliberate thoughts towards them. One was, "I hate you, I'm going to kill myself, I'm going to kill you". Other bottles had positive messages like, "I love you". The water was analysed under microscopes to see if there was any impact from the different messages, and the results at a molecular level were astounding. The water that had the negative messages was distorted, ugly and irregular. The bottles with beautiful, calming, and self-accepting messages on it was symmetrical, beautiful and harmonious. This was at a microscopic level but was clear to see.

We consider ourselves so much more "alive" than water, so imagine what this is doing to our bodies when we give ourselves messages of self-hate and run this low-level program of negative thoughts or resentment. At a cellular level, we are creating negativity, lack and distortion. This is why the forgiveness exercises are so important because it has the power to change you at that cellular level, where you love and accept yourself, no matter what. When you do that, you can accept wealth into your life.

"Everything we experience – no matter how unpleasant – comes into our lives to teach us something."
Iyanla Vanzant

One of my clients Tammy Guest is a naturopath and she used Dr Emoto's example to label her own herbal remedies. Instead of using words like "Headache" and

"Infertility" on her bottles, she's creating special labels infused with good intentions of "I'm well" and "I'm having a baby".

Seriously, you might be thinking – what does this have to do with money? *Everything*. Money is just a symbol for your life. It's a symbol of how well you treat yourself. Imagine that your income is exactly proportional to your level of self-love. What does that say about your current income? What would that say about your ability to love yourself unconditionally?

When I see women setting and then failing to hit financial goals, I know it's got nothing to do with money and everything to do healing and forgiveness. So please don't be stubborn about it. Just freaking do what you need to do to heal yourself. Pay the money. Even if you don't feel anything is really "wrong", go deeper and see what else you can uncover.

Heal Your Past Lives

In my quest to "throw everything at it", I also had an energetic clearing session with energy healer, Jenny Hobby who said that my poverty mentality came from at least 144 generations and helped me clear it. Imagine doing forgiveness work on your ancestors? Freaking powerful, right?

I also had a past life session with Melissa Kitto, of *Communicate with Angels* who told me a fascinating story of one of my past lives. I was a Japanese artist and sculptor hundreds of years ago, who refused to sell my art to the English who were coming to Japan in greater numbers. I was stubborn, wanting to be a purist and only sell to local people, stubbornly fighting for the ideal of "Japanese art for Japanese people". This decision sabotaged my business to the point of bankruptcy, and ultimately caused a lot of shame for my family. And whether or not you believe in past lives (I don't know if I do either), it was a really clear message for me in my present life. It was an allegory about being stubborn to the point of not allowing my talents to shine for the greatest good. I could relate to that story and forgave myself for past sabotages.

"People become really quite remarkable when they start believing that they can do things."
Norman Vincent Peale

Every meeting with an alternative therapy healer can be useful to reveal information about what habits you need to change. At my recent acupuncture appointment, my practitioner Mark asked me to tell him when the pain became too much. Straight away I steeled myself. I was going to withstand more pain than *anyone* else in his clinic. He was going to be so impressed. I caught myself in that moment and it became valuable information about my stubbornness. When I told Mark about my awareness, he said *"Denise, this isn't a test. The treatment doesn't have to be painful to be effective"*.

I thought that was profound. Healing doesn't have to be painful. It's just a tool so you can balance out what's not working and become more of yourself. And from a money point of view, when you give yourself permission to be perfect the way you are, you can become truly rich, both materially *and* spiritually.

Take Responsibility for the Bad Stuff

There is a concept within the Law of Attraction, that life is just a mirror. Everything that happens on the outside is just a reflection of everything you think and feel on the inside.

Remember, *thoughts become things*. Your thoughts will create your money situation, so you have to be so vigilant.

So unfortunately you also also need to take responsibility for any bad situation in your life. Only you can decide how you feel about it and what meaning you create in the world.

You can't overdose on decluttering old money "crap", so look around in your life and see where you consistently create negative emotion, so you can release it from your life.

For example, one of my clients, Kristen, had extremely negative emotions towards a billion dollar organisation that was privatising and buying up everything in her area. The general consensus was that the company was the enemy. Every time she read about it in the paper, she was pissed off, and even at dinner parties, it became a heated source of debate. She was expending so much energy on something that she had little control over, and although that energy might not seem like it's doing damage on your wealth consciousness, it totally is. It fuels your belief that *"rich people ruin the environment"* or that *"rich people are assholes who take what they want"*. It separates you from the wealthy and again, you will do everything in your power to repel money so you don't become an evil, uncaring rich bitch.

To overcome Kristen's negative mindset around the company and free her from her constantly angry thoughts, she did forgiveness work towards them. Yes, she felt like an idiot at first because she felt totally *justified* in her anger, but she immediately felt better. She also realised that she saw everything as a very black or white issue. She could now decide to take action towards it, by joining a lobby group or by rationally being involved in local community open forums without being angry about it all the time. She could *choose* her reaction consciously without her anger ruining her own life.

Doing forgiveness work towards *anything* you're angry about, gives you a completely different experience of it, whether it's politics or the economy.

If your thoughts create things, you have to take full responsibility for everything in your life and consciously choose a better thought. You can also reframe your anger as part of the decluttering process. If you want to get all woo-woo about it, maybe this is a cosmic lesson.

Maybe the unethical CEO or the dick-head politician is here to teach us something. Imagine that soul's contract was to come to Earth, play this antagonistic role to show us what could happen with the bad side of wealth. They volunteered for that at a soul level. That's not a fun assignment, so we can genuinely forgive and love them for it at a soul level. I never condone unethical behaviour but I forgive it and release it as a valuable lesson.

Kristen and I looked at the billion dollar organisation as being sent to Earth to teach her something about wealth. When she thought of it this way she was able to have some compassion towards the organisation and its directors, without condoning their behaviour. She was able to turn her negative thoughts to ones of empathy and kindness. It was a really important lesson because if she had stayed fixated on the negative the Universe would pick up on those negative vibrations and deliver more of the same to her in the form of her favourite sabotage. You can only feel one emotion at any one time and when you're consumed with anger and resentment, there's no room for abundance.

Are you willing to accept that you have brought these negative situations into your reality for a reason?

Have a go at doing some forgiveness work on organisations and people you hate with a passion *even if it feels stupid*. You can transform hate and resentment into love and empathy. My guess is that you will feel peaceful, happier and more productive to take action on your dreams. And that's true wealth.

Chapter Summary

- Forgiveness is the tool to release you from the past and allow you to be rich
- No money memory is too big or small to clear, everything is symbolic
- EFT will change your life, try it daily and see what changes in your life
- Throw everything at it – something will work and will free you from your negative self beliefs around money

For a gorgeous forgiveness mantra poster, make sure you sign up for your book bonuses at www.GetRichLuckyBitch.com.

Create Big Money Goals

"All sins are forgiven once you start making a lot of money."
Rupaul

Can I ask you a personal question? We're friends now, you can tell me. I won't laugh, be shocked or think you're up yourself. Lucky Bitch land is an extremely safe space to share and brag. Here goes:

How much do you want to earn next year?

That question might be easy for you or make you want to put down this book and head to the fridge. Most women when pressed can pull a big number out of their butt and I either find that the number is wayyyyy too small, or is crazy unrealistic. I've met women who have only ever earned a couple of thousand dollars in their business and their very next goal is a million. I've also worked with women who just hope to earn the same amount of money as last year and can't imagine how they could ever earn more. Either way, you're in the right place.

This whole book is about getting you comfortable with

earning more money, no matter what your starting point. It's also about being comfortable with talking about money and shouting out loud to the Universe exactly what you want in your life, no matter how simple or outrageous.

So, that's why I asked your income goal. You've got to get comfortable talking about it. You can't have goal shame and expect to manifest it easily. I hear this all the time: *"I'm almost embarrassed to tell you"*. Don't be embarrassed, it's only a goal.

It's time to get really clear with the Universe so it knows exactly what to deliver to you. No mixed messages and no goal shame.

The Simple Every Day Exercise That Will Change Your Life

The simplest way of manifesting your goals is by writing them down every day, including a goal of *exactly* how much you want to make. It's a simple way to keep your goals top of mind and the Universe will start to rearrange itself for you when it knows exactly what you want.

Many books, articles and studies have been done on the power of goal setting, so listen to this lucky bitch life coach and just do it, ok?

Writing out your goals every day would be awesome. Every other day will create amazing things and even just doing them once a week or month will put you so far ahead of the game it's not funny. Most people don't even write down their New Year's resolutions. The act of writing them is important because it's a declaration out of your head and onto the paper, plus the intention behind them actually requires you to think about what you want.

Making that decision is the first step. I know it can sound really fucking obvious and it's not a huge big revelation. *"Write down your goals, that's your genius advice? I want my money back Denise!"*

Hey listen – I live and breathe this stuff and I don't always remember to write down my goals every day, but when I do, my money manifesting goes through the roof. Hearing it, agreeing that it's important and actually ***doing*** something about it makes all the difference. It's almost 10pm at night and I'm yet to write down my goals today. So, I just took two minutes and wrote them down. Simple.

You don't have to write them down perfectly every time, just doodle them down on paper. They don't have to be perfectly laminated either. They can change daily if you want, but the process of doing it regularly means that your most important goals will be revealed because you are consistent in writing them. You will probably forget to write out your unimportant goals overtime, so don't worry about them.

Goal setting stimulates that part of your brain called the Reticular Activating System, which basically controls mental alertness and functions as a filter to categorize the most important information at any one time. You can train your brain to choose what's important by regular and consistent goal setting. It will help you to recognise opportunities because you're more conditioned to actually *see* them.

When you know exactly WHAT you're working towards, you will start to act in more positive ways towards your goals, because you've trained yourself over time to believe them. The belief fuels the action. Many "coincidences" and synchronicities will occur and the

HOW takes care of itself. People will start to call *you* a lucky bitch.

"Don't simply dismiss a coincidence and let it drift away. Life is totally interconnected. These unusual 'things' are simply connections that surprise you because you aren't used to seeing life except in fragments. Now it is beginning to piece itself together."
Deepak Chopra

I heard once that the difference between a millionaire and a billionaire is that the billionaire writes their goals down ***twice*** a day. That's really freaking motivating, so take two minutes now and write down some goals. They don't have to be perfect. Just do it.

Remember Denise Austin, the fitness guru from the 80s? Her slogan was *"Do it every day, do it with Denise"*. That's what I want you to remember. Goal setting is an everyday thing if you want to manifest like a mofo. It's easy and it's free.

That's why you should always have your money tracking sheet to hand - either as a printed out document or open on your computer at all times. You will constantly be reminded of your money goals and how you're working towards them each and every day. Your free Lucky Bitch money tracking sheets also have space for your monthly goals and current affirmation, but you must fill it out for the magic to work. Don't forget to download yours, using the password LOVEMONEY from www.GetRichLuckyBitch.com.

When I was in my twenties, my goal was to be a

millionaire by thirty. It had a nice ring to it, right? I know I didn't hit that goal because I had such massive unresolved lessons to learn, so my twenties were less about money making and more about forgiveness, clearing and decluttering my emotions, fears and self-worth.

So my new goal in all transparency is to be a millionaire by 35. One of my mentors, Ali Brown was a millionaire by 35, so it seems like a good goal. The difference now compared to before was that I actually believe I'll achieve it *and* I have a plan to get it done. I know exactly how it can happen plus I have this amazing set of tools to declutter any fear or resistance to making it happen (which WILL come up). Each time I increase my income, I go back to step one of my manifesting formula because I know there's more to learn.

"Money is such an amazing teacher: What you choose to do with your money shows whether you are truly powerful or powerless."
Suze Orman

When I first ran my money Bootcamp, I thought the information would only be valuable to women who were really struggling to earn good money. What I realised is that the lessons are the same at every level of income. I was shocked to see women who were earning six figures and close to being millionaires who still wanted to work on this stuff. For some reason, I thought that at some point, there was no more to learn. Big mistake. There is *always* more to learn and it doesn't mean that you are stupid, slow or unworthy. It's just the journey.

So when women started joining my bootcamp, it was

interesting that they were all at different stages of wealth, but they all thought the exercises were transformational… the *same* exercises. Some people were in crisis mode and were hearing it for the first time, others just wanted to try out new techniques to go to the next level of abundance. The women who were already successful know the power of goal setting and know there is always more to learn about yourself.

At this point in your journey to get rich, you might be starting to get frustrated if actual money hasn't shown up for you yet. You've been decluttering like crazy and you set a massive goal and now you're like *"Where's my* cash, *mofo?"*

Keep an eye out for symbols like little coins, or pictures of money, or how much you're getting stuff for free. These are usually signs from the Universe that the money is on its way. But that could still leave you wondering, *"Why hasn't it come?"*

You might be even manifesting extra bills and this sucks when it happens, but trust me, it's happening for a reason. It's as though everything in your life that isn't aligned to money is bubbling up to the surface. All your past mistakes or bad habits around money are showing up. This is exactly like when you start to take care of your skin and you get a temporary breakout. You might think it's a shitty reward for suddenly being so virtuous but it's because you're uncovering all the crap under the surface. Better out than in! Don't give up.

This temporary crap-fest or money drought can be cured by *specificity*. Money *loves* clarity. The Universe is like the most loyal and enthusiastic dog in the world. It wants to serve you, but you've got to tell it what you want.

I saw this great documentary once about this incredibly well-trained dog who could identify thousands of different items. Her owner scattered at least 100 different toys randomly around a live stage and then asked the dog to fetch things. *"Bring the parrot. Good girl! Now bring the rooster."* This dog bounded around the stage to collect the items and only got one thing wrong… out of a hundred. It was the most fun game ever for that dog, she loved being of service.

Now imagine the Universe is like that dog. It's waiting there with tail wagging, waiting expectantly for an instruction. As soon as you say the word, it will rush around, find it and bring it to you. Now – it might not happen instantaneously. But the more you train the Universe to serve you – the faster it will happen. My six months all expenses paid trip took six months to manifest, but I've also manifested large sums of money within 24 hours. When your manifesting muscles are well trained, it's *easy* but it's not permanent. It requires daily action, including goal setting.

Back to the dog analogy. You don't train a dog to that level of obedience with *one* training session and then you give up because you don't feel like it anymore. It can take days, weeks, months and years of repetitive training, repetitive commands and lots of positive reinforcement to learn different skills.

So, train the Universe by repeating your goals daily and acknowledge the Universe by tracking your money daily. It could feel tedious and unrewarding at first and that's why most people are not outrageously successful – they don't have the patience to continue. I've had many goals that I've abandoned because I wasn't willing to put in the work and gave up. By "work", I mean the daily commitment to making it happen on a practical and metaphysical level.

I told you I'd be honest and it sounds harsh, but not everyone is going to be rich. Most people say they *want* to be rich, but ask them their goals and they have no idea. Ask them to do forgiveness work and they say it's too hard or unnecessary. They'll say "I tried that once and it didn't work". Ask them ten things they could do to earn money right now and they'll say *"I dunno. I can't think of anything"*. They'll just buy a lottery ticket instead.

Our community of Lucky Bitches take responsibility for our money. We're always looking for what we can do next and we strive to get even clearer on what we want.

So, when you're feeling frustrated, make sure you've given your money something really specific to flow to with this really simple exercise.

The Only Goal Setting Exercise You Need

This is a simple exercise that has the power to change your life. I do it at least once a month but when I do it weekly, it's unbelievably powerful.

Introducing the **Be, Do & Have** exercise.

It's just a simple way to define exactly what you would like to Be, Do and Have in your life. Duh - pretty much exactly as it describes! I love this exercise, because it makes you define your goal setting from different angles.

You might think you can't repeat this one daily but you totally can, although I like to do it weekly. It's fun to re-write the list and see what different goals you come up with. I have them scattered all over the place, in old diaries and on scrap paper and it's fun to find them months or years later and realise that you can tick them off. Make sure you put a date on them so you can see how far you've come. It doesn't have to be perfect. Just do it.

The sooner you define what you want, the quicker the Universe will deliver it to you. Trust me.

As you do this exercise, imagine that you have a magic pen and everything that you write on your paper is going to come true in the next six months. How cool would that be?

Sometimes when I'm doing this exercise at a workshop, I have people who sit there and stare into the distance not knowing what they want. If that happens to you just put your pen to the paper and see what comes out. Sometimes if you just write one random thing more ideas will flood to you. Don't overthink it, just write. What do you want to be doing, where do you want to be living, what do you want to have in your life over the next year?

It always keeps your goals in the front of your mind. It's like creating a dream board but with words.

To take this exercise to the next level, write down numerical values next to each of the goals, so you know how much it is actually going to *cost* you to have that big dream house or car. Try not to limit or moderate yourself even if your dream is to own a million dollar house, just do the calculations and find out how much it would cost.

Dream big because anything is possible if you define it. Remember your reality is 100% negotiable, you are in charge and you can choose what you end up with. And of course you do this by always sending out those positive vibrations, bypass all that negativity, and remain really focused on your goals. I'm like a broken record - declutter and forgive.

Ok, let me tell you an awesome story about the power of the Be, Do, Have list and why it's important to write it out regularly.

For the last few years, one of my goals was to buy a multi-million dollar house overlooking the ocean. I wrote this on my goal list so many times and I did all the tools I give you in this book. I even had the exact one picked out. I visited it all the time, pretending to drive up as if it was already mine. I had the picture of it as my iPhone screensaver, I used the address as my password. The weird thing is that Mark's boss bought the house next door, so I felt like that was a sign from the Universe that this house was important because suddenly I was one step removed from it.

I was starting to get impatient, so I made a tiny tweak to my Be, Do & Have list, that was entirely unintentional but changed my life. One day, I realised that I was writing "Live in a multi-million dollar house", rather than my usual "Buy". Without realising it, I sent into the Universe a different intention, with a completely different chain of events.

You see - when you declare a big intention, the Universe sets off like that enthusiastic dog to fetch it for you. If it's a big goal, it requires lots of subtle changes to make it happen (imagine a complicated set of cogs and wheels working behind the scenes). Although you don't see anything changing, things *are* moving, however slowly at first. However, I was spending more time on the HOW, rather than the WHAT.

When I focused my attention on actually *living* in a

multi-million dollar house, my brain stopped worrying about house deposits, credit scores and interest rates and came up with more creative solutions instead.

I realised that in Australia with interest rates so high (around 8%), it can be cheaper to rent than to buy. So we set out to find our dream house. It only took us 6 weeks from changing my intention to actually living in our new multi-million dollar apartment overlooking the water. The rent is about the same as the mortgage on a house a quarter of its value. We didn't have to save for years, we didn't have to pay closing costs and no long term commitment. No, I won't own it but I don't have to worry about repairs, rates or market value either. For us, it was the ultimate instant gratification solution, and it came from changing just one word on my goal list. Powerful stuff!

Remember, I'm not a financial advisor. I can't tell you to rent instead of buying a house. You might have more patience than me. But if you have a similar goal, then look around and see what's out there and find out exactly how much it would cost to live in your dream house.

Or look at any dream. You could get it quicker than you think if you change the rules of how you think you could get it.

I knew that I couldn't go to the next level of income in our previous flat. It was small, my office was also the spare bedroom and it was time to graduate from that place to something spectacular. The energy wouldn't be right with my clients, even if they couldn't actually see where I was working. It felt like a big symbolic leap forward and a massive upgrade.

The hilarious thing is that as soon as we made the decision, my income practically doubled overnight. Even

Mark's income increased. Now, every day as I create my business and work on my goals (even as I'm writing this), I'm overlooking one of the best views in town. I regularly see dolphins outside my window. I suddenly have other things on my Be, Do & Have list (a huge walk in closet and a weirdly Virgo thing - multiple laundry baskets for colour coordinating our dirty laundry). I had my best month ever after living in this house for just four weeks and the following month was even better. We could more than afford it when we actually looked at the actual price instead of day dreaming about it.

The point is twofold, sometimes your goals cost less than you think and secondly, the Universe always has more creative ways to give you what you want, so don't get hung up on *how* you'll manifest your goals. Your job right now is just to clarify them and declutter any fears that surface.

The Worst Case Scenario

One of the reasons women don't want to commit to writing down their goals is fear of failure. *"What if I commit to a goal and then it doesn't come true?"* Or what if you commit to a goal and then you suddenly got everything your heart desired, what would happen then? Would you freak out? Would other people hate you?

Take a look at one of those goals that you're a too afraid to write down and lets brainstorm all the crazy, terrible and downright ridiculous things that could happen. Seriously, what is the absolute worst thing you can think of if you were to achieve that goal?

This might seem like a counter intuitive exercise, especially for a Lucky Bitch, but it's hugely important and gives you valuable information that you can declutter and forgive. Remember, you can't get through this with stubborn will power. The only way is to declutter the junk and make your life easy, to blow up the boulders in your river of abundance. Those fears are already living inside you, we're just going to verbalise them.

Let me give you an example. Say you wanted to increase your salary to $100k in the next six months (or a million, whatever). Think about all of the unintended negative consequences of that coming true. When I ask my clients for their unexpected fears, usually they say, "*Nothing. That would be amazing*". So I probe a little further and wait patiently until I hear things like:

- *My friends might expect me to pick up the bill all the time. That would suck.*
- *Someone's going to ask me for a loan and it's going to feel awkward and uncomfortable when I say no.*
- *I'll have to pay more taxes. I hate taxes.*
- *I'll have to give money to my crazy, dead-beat brother/cousin.*
- *My ex-husband will cut off the child support. What a fucker, he'll love doing that to spite me.*
- *I'll fuck it up like I always do and end up broke again, so what's the point?*
- *I'll lose my benefits so I'll be no better off.*
- *I'll probably spend it all and get in trouble with the tax department.*
- *I'll waste it on stupid things for the kids and they'll become spoilt little brats.*

Be crazy and creative with it and go as deep as you can. Come up with as many negative reasons, little ones, big ones, totally ridiculous ones; whatever you can think of. Some of them are just unvoiced fears but others can hit you hard, because it reminds you of something unresolved, like an old memory you need to forgive.

I make my clients keep going. What else? Ok, what else? Even after they say *"I'm done. I can't think of anything else"*, we keep going.

Eventually after about twenty reasons, you'll get one or two that really hit home. Bingo. You'll realise that you are actually purposefully holding yourself back from earning more because of these fears. Yes, *purposefully* repelling money. There is a part of you that is so scared by earning more that you will do anything to keep yourself safe, including sabotaging your goals. Your ego literally will not allow it. That's why drastically increasing your income feels hard if you haven't done your decluttering work. You have hit a self-imposed wall and you can't successfully fight yourself.

"I love money. Got myself a $300 pair of socks. Got a fur sink. An electric dog polisher. A gasoline powered turtleneck sweater. And, I bought some dumb stuff, too."
Steve Martin

Take an objective look at what you've written as your worst case scenarios. Really step back and see where all this is coming from. They could be negative self-beliefs stemming from your past experiences with your goals in the past.

Do a little digging so you have specific incidences to declutter and forgive. Maybe you might have seen someone in your family who had to work really hard to earn their wealth, and as a consequence their relationships or health suffered. Maybe you had a rich family member who had to lend money all the time and you're scared that that will happen to you. You're worried about saying no and have people think you're a bitch.

Brainstorm *all* of the extremely negative, truly *worst* things that could happen if you were rich. You'll never see your kids because you're working so hard, or you will divorce your husband because he's emasculated by your wealth, or that your deadbeat cousin will hit you up for a loan to pay his meth dealer.

By writing down the worst consequences of becoming wealthy you will see that there is a really high chance that those things will never actually happen, but it also gives you some work to do.

Once Bootcamp participant Cecelia *finally* had her goal list down on paper, her next stumbling block was *"How the hell am I going to do this?"*

We did this unintended negative consequences exercise on her goal to own a beach house. Of course, at first, she's like *"I can't think of anything Denise, I've wanted this beach house my whole life"*.

I said "Humour me. There must be some drawbacks to owning this beach house". After much prodding and suggestions, they started pouring out of her. The expense, the obligation, the unwanted guests, the repairs, etc. Work on those fears before you even worry about the how. That is the Universe's job.

Naming your fears isn't showing weakness or telling the Universe you don't really want it. It's just a temporary elimination round. You don't even have to come up with solutions to combat each fear. You just do some EFT and release it to the Universe. Sometimes the exercise gives you practical information that you can work on, for example, knowing how much you need to save for a deposit, or getting insurance to cover potential losses. Do anything you need to do to feel safe.

"My mother always said don't marry for money, divorce for money."
Wendy Liebman

I asked this same question on Facebook. See if you relate to anything and add it to your forgiveness list.

"What would be the worst thing that could happen if you were suddenly rich?"

"Feeling like I have to leave people behind or some people wouldn't understand where I'm going and we'll have to part ways." – Jia Ni Teo

"Getting bored with it!" – Cheryl Bigus

"I would end up in trashy magazines and have articles written about me saying 'Look at the state of her. Has she had Botox? Headlines like – 'Visible batwings while Michelle shopped in Coles this Sunday morning'." – Michelle Marie McGrath

"That it was not what I thought it would be." – Samantha Leith

"The people who suddenly appear, who didn't give you the time of day, when you appear more successful than

them." – Michelle Hunter

"The potential to have to choose career over love." – Kellie Czajkowski

"I would have to work a lot harder, be innovative all the time and watch my weight, lest the tabloids and Twitter also unleash their cruel barbs at my derriere!" – Dawn Lewis

"Fear of fame, and losing my privacy." – Mercedes Maidana

"Demands upon me and my time, people trying to dictate to me how I create my art." – Kristine Schroeder

"Having to let go of some people in my life." – Jennifer Kent

"Screwing up – fear of everyone saying I told you so!" – Charlotte Gonzalez

"Spoiling my kids by buying lavish gifts for them!" – Michelle Goddard

My clients are surprised when I get them to do this exercise because they think you have to be positive all the time to achieve your goals. That's bullshit and it's part of the perfection mentality that *"I must be perfect and pure in thought before I deserve anything"*.

This exercise gives us very specific and real fears to declutter, so the more creative you can be the better. I like to really dig deep with my clients and let them voice their deepest and most embarrassing fears. If you don't allow yourself to admit them, you won't break forward to the next level because you'll be unconsciously protecting yourself. Remember, everything happens for your highest good. You are ALWAYS protected.

Here's what you do next:

Look at each negative fear or unintended consequence of becoming rich and ask yourself, "is there anything I need to forgive? Are there any memories or emotions I need to clear around this?".

Also do some EFT on it and say:

"Even though I'm going to ruin my marriage with my financial success,
Even though my kids are never going to see me...

...I deeply and completely love and accept myself".

Voicing those little fears, even if they're completely irrational, releases their hold on you and you can feel good about becoming rich. It gives you freedom to set really big and bold goals, knowing that nothing bad will happen to you.

You will be free to manifest your goals because it will feel safe again. What happens if you don't take my advice? You'll die alone as a crazy cat lady.

No, I'm joking! Quite simply, you're going to self-sabotage to protect yourself from those unwanted and scary scenarios. Giving voice to them will release their hold on you.

Getting Goal Setting "Right"

Remember that those things you write down on your Bed, Do & Have list are not set in stone. You can always change them or let them evolve over time. Goals just train the Universe to serve you.

Some women procrastinate writing their goals (or take any action) because of the fear of getting it wrong. One of my clients, Cecelia told me she was procrastinating doing her list because she thought she only had one chance at it and didn't want to mess it up.

Really what is the worst that could happen? You use up a bit of paper, no big deal. Nobody is going to die. Even if you use your fanciest linen paper notebook and the most expensive fountain pen, it doesn't matter if you fuck it up. Start again. I've screwed up the first page in a new journal, ripped it out and started again. Like farts, goals are better out than in, so release them into the world and onto some paper today!

Remember the magic is in the *repetition*, not how nice it's going to look on the paper. You don't have to laminate it. Perfect calligraphy won't manifest it quicker.

Fears are common when you try and set a bigger goal than normal. What will separate you from the average person is how quickly you recognise the fear, declutter it and move on.

I had a client who wanted to make $10,000 in one month. The most she had ever made was a few thousand, so her fears were on turbo-drive.

"I started stressing about having no education in marketing and sales; that I wasn't a professional negotiator. I felt that if I was going put in 150%, then I would be really disappointed if I didn't reach my goal. I was afraid of not getting what I wanted," Jess said.

I encouraged Jess to do some EFT on her fear of not being good enough, because those thoughts were derailing her from reaching her goal, not her experience level or how badly she wanted it. Also, the goal was too big a stretch and it was freaking her out. You have to actually *believe* you can do it, even if the thought scares you. Set your goals in increments until you have the confidence to make a big leap.

It might sound like I'm making goal setting really complicated, but actually, this makes it easier. It's a hell of a lot easier to manifest your goal when you have little to no energetic, mental or practical impediments in the way.

It's okay to work on your list over time, refine it, perfect it and change it. It will no doubt evolve as you work towards living your own version of a First Class life. Remember that the difference between a millionaire and a billionaire is that the billionaire writes her goals down twice a day. So just do it. Now.

Your Income is NEVER Fixed

I recently had a potential client contact me to ask for a longer payment plan. Like many female entrepreneurs, a request around negotiating payment brought up a lot of fears for me around wanting to be fair, inclusive, accommodating, and not wanting people to think I'm a bitch.

I thought about it for a few days and told her I would accept smaller payments every two weeks instead of a bigger payment once a month. On the surface, that might seem like a pointless gesture, but I know that when you start working on your money energy, you'll start to manifest more money straight away.

In her response she said she was on a fixed income and needed the longer payment plan. I wanted to tell her. "You only have a fixed ***assumption*** about your income. If you believe your income is fixed you will perpetuate it forever."

Being in business brings up all your money boundaries better than any personal development conference ever could. But that's why I love working with entrepreneurs, we can move quickly because we are constantly being tested!

Your income is unlimited. Your potential is unlimited.

It's easy to justify to ourselves why we can't have what we want. We become more fixated on WHY we can't have outrageous success and restrict ourselves to a little box. I've done it before too, but it's a bullshit excuse.

I told myself that I couldn't be rich because of all sorts of random excuses. I was too short, not pretty enough, not skinny enough, not well educated enough, Australian, a woman, I had a big butt…

You can only make those big leaps in income by ripping apart the box that only you alone have put yourself in. The self-imposed label that says, "I can only earn this and no more". If you think $100k is out of reach or you'll never reach a million, that's exactly what will happen. You don't need to know exactly how you'll get there right now, just allow yourself to dream it and become a ruthless declutterer of every negative self-belief standing in your way.

Be aware of what labels you've put on yourself, thinking that you have to wait until you're the perfect weight or more organised (or whatever), until you're "allowed" to be rich.

I recently had a client tell me that she needed to take a writing course as her next step, despite the fact that she had a popular blog she updated every day. It wasn't true, she was just using it as an excuse as to why she couldn't make more money. It was a minor distraction that we recognised straight away.

When I started making money in my business, I remember thinking I should get elocution lessons before I really became successful, just in case people didn't like my voice. What a dumbshit excuse. It would only stop me making money if I believed that it would.

What excuses are you using?

Give Yourself Permission to Be Rich Now

Some women live their lives back to front. They want the money first, so they can *do* what they want. Then they'll *be* the person they've always wanted to be. Happier, less worried, perfect. It actually works the other way round. If you let yourself BE who you already are, money will just enhance that. It will give you the freedom to DO what you want and HAVE anything your heart desires.

It's actually more important in the short term to *feel* rich, than to actually be rich, as one usually follows the other. Otherwise, how rich is enough to give yourself permission to feel good? How will you know when to stop accumulating money and enjoy it? When are you allowed to be happy?

If I were to tell you my actual income right now, some of you would be impressed, some would be intimidated and some would be like, *"Is that all?"*. My barometer of financial success right now is that I feel rich; I have enough money to travel and live my life the way I want to, and I'm still motivated to strive for new goals because I want to be a hell of a lot richer! You can aim to be better and still feel good about it.

I was attending the fabulous Marie Forleo's *Rich, Happy & Hot* event in New York with, Def Jam Records founder, Russell Simmons as the headline speaker. Now, maybe because I grew up in Australia or maybe because my musical tastes run more to Broadway tunes than hip hop, I had no idea who "Uncle Rush" even was. However, I was compelled by his philosophies on money and his incredible book *Super Rich*.

Open question time came around and a young woman came up to the microphone and said;

"Uncle Rush, I'm doing really well in my business but it's never enough. I grew up poor and now I feel like I have to hustle all the time. I'm worried that I'll never *be happy with what I've got"*.

His answer blew my mind:

Nothing will ever feed the poverty of your own soul.

Basically, his message was, "You're right. It will never be enough if you believe that".

You have to decide NOW that you are enough. You are smart enough, pretty enough, clever enough, ready enough. You can be richer starting today, if you're brave enough to define exactly what you want.

"No matter where you're from or what you've done,
you're never stuck in a particular circumstance,
relationship, or cycle unless you say you are."
Russell Simmons

I find that my own income is rising rapidly now because I'm finally being true to who I am and I know what I want.

I used to try and be nice to everyone. I had a few people send me feedback about my occasional swearing because it bothered them. I didn't quite tell them to "fuck off", but I didn't worry about it either. It's their opinion and they can find someone else to hang out with. I'm sorry if you don't like it, but you can find heaps of other non-swearing books about money.

I had someone send me a lecture because I used the word "vagina" in a tweet, because they said it wasn't professional and I'd probably lose followers. After I decided not to stress about it, I had a coaching session with S.J Tierney, the author of *The Vagina Buffet* to help her with marketing her book. Her book says the word vagina about a million times and it's awesome. Nobody can tell you to change. There's always going to be someone who loves it and someone who hates it.

Who Do You Want To Be?

I have always wanted to be wealthy. Even though I didn't hit my goal of being a millionaire by thirty, I know now it's because I was trying to do things that weren't in alignment with who I am.

My first eBook was titled *Internet Dating Tips for Men* and I was a little embarrassed. I didn't want to tell people about it so of course it wasn't that successful. If I had been passionate about it I would've been happy to put more of my time and effort into promoting it, talking about it and pitching it so maybe it would've been more of a success. But because it wasn't really 'me' it died a slow death.

I spent most of my twenties doing a bunch of random jobs. I did a medical experiment to pay my university tuition. I did commission-only sales in supermarkets. I did telesales. I even worked for a phone sex company for six months. I understand why I did it at the time and thought it was *hilarious* but I'm sad I didn't believe I could use my talents in better ways for a pay cheque. I had the skills to do what I'm doing now but I just wasn't being true to myself so I wasted my time in jobs that made me feel awful and didn't really bring in the big bucks that I wanted.

If I had followed my dreams and been really focused on my goal and knew earlier in my life that I wanted to be a coach, author and mentor, then I could've been much further on my path to becoming a millionaire. A lot of that comes with maturity and experience and I wasn't ready to do my forgiveness work.

I find most women really do know deep down what they want to do. It's probably always been there in your childhood, you just have emotional "stuff" in the way. When you clear that, you give yourself permission to earn money in an easy, safe and beautiful way.

I know now that money just enhances who you already are and you don't have to change yourself fundamentally to get it.

"If you're given a choice between money and sex appeal, take the money. As you get older, the money will become your sex appeal."
Katherine Hepburn

Define What Wealth Really Means to You

As you start to refine your goal list, you will build a detailed picture of exactly what you desire in your life.

Being wealthy means different things for different people. You might not want a Jaguar, or a BMW, or to be a millionaire. All you want is to have peace of mind and to be happy. That's cool.

But you need to define what 'peace of mind' actually looks like because it's too vague to be a useful goal. A goal like *"I want more time"* can't manifest because everyone has the exact same amount of time in the day. The Universe can't give that to you, so it's a waste of goal setting energy.

Let's break it down. "I want to have more time with my kids". What does that look like to you? Do you want to spend a whole day with them on Saturday or do you literally want to spend all day every day with your kids?

Think about what needs to happen for you to be able to spend an extra two hours a day with your kids. Maybe it means you need to get a cleaner, hire an assistant in your business or have a certain amount of money coming in so the bills get paid without worry. Maybe you just want to be there for mealtimes or bedtimes. Get specific.

I set a goal this year of "have more fun" as I spent a lot of last year being an anti-social hermit. But I knew I had to get more specific, so I came up with some simple things that sounded fun, like:

- *Try pole dancing classes*
- *Make a dance video for my business*
- *Be involved in a flash mob*
- *Go to Mindvalley's Awesomeness Fest*
- *Write a book about zombies*

Drill down all your vague goals so they become more specific. This particularly applies to goals like "be less stressed" or "have peace of mind". Be specific and choose just one thing that would cause you less stress, peace of mind or create more fun in your life. Just one thing.

"Money frees you from doing things you dislike.
Since I dislike doing nearly everything,
money is handy."
Groucho Marx

Maybe being wealthy means you are able to travel the world. Instead of just writing 'travel the world' on your list, write down the places you want to visit. Maybe you want to spend a white Christmas drinking glühwein in Germany, or visit Japan when the cherry blossoms are blooming, or you want to go storm chasing in America during the hurricane season. (I want to swim with dolphins in Hawaii wearing a mermaid tail). Specific details like that will help to build your vision into reality.

Money is just a tool to help us get what we want.

One of the most common things women put on their list is to be a good mother, daughter or wife and be happy in their relationships. To get those kind of goals concrete and clearly defined can be hard, but it can be done.

Writing coach Kris Emery said she wanted to be a better daughter to her parents. A nice goal, but virtually useless from a Law of Attraction perspective. So we brainstormed specific and measurable ways to do that, for example, she could call her parents more regularly or remember birthdays but she realised that she was holding herself back from what she really wanted to do.

"If I was really dreaming big and being honest with myself I'd like to visit them more regularly, but I almost couldn't believe that would happen so I didn't put 'a flight to the UK once a year' down on my list," Kris said.

By putting this specific goal of flying home to visit her parents once a year Kris had something positive to focus on and work towards. It's a much more concrete goal than her original one, and it is one that helps her to achieve her overall aim of being a better daughter.

It also now has a numerical figure on it. She'll know roughly how much a flight costs each year to the UK and now the Universe has something to work with. Instead of chasing an arbitrary desire to be "better", she can now feel good about achieving a weekly phone call and a flight home once a year.

"Money isn't everything...but it ranks right up there with oxygen."
Rita Davenport

I believe the reluctance to take vague goals to the next level of specificity is that some goals sound nicer in our heads but feel like a drag in reality. Ask yourself how willing you are to make it happen in the real world?

Do you *really* want to call your parents every day and spend *every* minute with your kids? Nope, so pick something you can easily achieve so you feel like a winner. Achievement breeds more achievement, and money follows good feelings.

You know that quote, "you can't buy happiness"? Well, it's kind of true because it's a stupid unquantifiable goal. But you can buy a gorgeous teapot and fancy tea leaves that will make you feel happy for an afternoon. You can buy a new purse that will increase your happiness every time you use it. You can buy an hour by yourself by hiring a babysitter, so you have time to do something that makes you feel happy. You can buy a day in a spa to feel relaxed. You can donate money to charity and feel good all day. Money can create happiness but in itself, it's not a great goal.

Unless you can quantify it into a SMART goal; Specific, Measurable, Achievable, Realistic and Time-bound, forget it and let yourself off the hook. It's not necessary to be happy all the time to be an incredible manifester. Strive for consistency, not perfection.

The mattress company Forty Winks has a simple shouty slogan, "Get a better bed!". Short and to the point. Here's mine:

Get a better goal!

I'm just going to start randomly shouting that at people. No more Mrs Nice Girl. If you're on a call with me and tell me your goal is to be "happy", expect me to yell that at you.

Get super specific about your goals and the Universe will start arranging happy coincidences and synchronicities just for you, which is super awesome when it happens.

If your goals are looking a little flaky, define what you need to achieve them. For example:

"Get fitter" turns into:

- Be able to touch my toes
- Lose 5 kgs by June
- Be able to run 5 minutes without stopping on a treadmill

Think of these as mini goals which all add up to you attaining everything on your Be, Do & Have list. Plus, you'll feel like you're getting somewhere when you can actually define it.

Break down that useless goal into tiny bite-sized chunks and the Universe will run to help you and fetch what you need. How will you know?

You'll find a pole dancing flyer in the mail. You'll see a sale on flights back home. You'll even start to see the money manifest to pay for it all. Why? Because you've given the money something specific to flow to. You've put a "price tag on happiness".

Chapter Summary

- Money loves clarity so define what wealth means to you
- Your income is never fixed. You are only restricted by the size of your dream

Action - tweet me one of the goals you're working on to @denisedt (be warned, I might tweet back "get a better goal" if it's not specific enough!

$

Feel Good About Your Money Now

"Stormy or sunny days, glorious or lonely nights, I maintain an attitude of gratitude. If I insist on being pessimistic, there is always tomorrow. Today I am blessed"
Maya Angelou

Feeling good about your money is more important than the size of your bank account and that's not always easy when the reality is less than spectacular.

I'm not going to lie. When you want to manifest a huge goal or break through to a new income level, sometimes you have to put in 150%.

Not everyone has the fortitude to continue through the temporary bumps along the road to outrageous success. Sometimes this just seems like too much hard work, especially if you don't pull it off. Not everyone has the guts to keep going.

Now, it's not *hard* work like having to sweat down in the mines or become a meth dealer (I'm watching a lot of *Breaking Bad* at the moment, so it's my default definition of a bad job), but it requires a constant vigilance that the average person can't be bothered to do. But I know you're different. I know how much you want to be richer and I know you're willing to study, learn, declutter and put in the "work" to make it happen, no matter what.

When I was manifesting my six months all- expenses-paid trip, I was super vigilant with my thoughts and actions; I really became the ultimate reverse paranoid because honestly, that's what it takes to manifest something out of the ordinary.

What would happen if you decided to feel great about your money NOW, no matter the current reality? This doesn't require super intelligence. In fact, dumb blissful ignorance would work best.

You just have to be willing to change.

I get people who email me all the time, who tell me their stories of being broke and although they think they are asking for solutions, they aren't really ready to hear them. Some people want the Universe to shift and change for them but aren't willing to change their state *now* and believe something different can happen *today*. I'll tell them everything I'm telling you now, go and forgive every bad financial mistake you've ever made, and they'll write back and say, "How can I win the lottery?"

Le sigh.

This is super *super* important. You have to feel good about your money *now*, or you never will. If you don't try and feel wealthy now with what you have, you won't feel wealthy with a million dollars. That is why people who win the lottery usually lose it within five years. They aren't aligned to that level of wealth. It's why the rich CEO works even harder and longer hours so he can get even richer. It's never enough.

I know the feeling. Almost every month this past year has broken new records for me. I have to remind myself that it's okay to feel safe and rich no matter what. I have to be vigilant in my thoughts otherwise, no matter how much money I make, I don't feel rich.

So start practicing now, because it starts with your everyday thoughts and feelings. Seriously - you've got to almost brainwash yourself (i.e. wash your brain) with as much positivity as possible and police yourself when it comes to verbalising anything to the contrary.

Here's what my mentor Sandy Forster, author of *Wildly Wealthy Fast* has to say about this;

"Watch your self-talk. When you share publicly and use a lot of words like: desperate, don't know what to do, scared, give up etc. then what must you be saying to YOURSELF in your head 24 hours a day? **Your self-talk and your feelings are what create**.

Become conscious and very aware of what you are saying to yourself about money every single day - because that is your ORDER for more of the same. When you shift your energy, your vibration and your point of attraction EVERYTHING will change - believe me, I know it, I have lived it and I have transformed it. I know it's possible for ALL OF YOU too!"

If you give up and start to go back to your old negative ways of thinking and speaking, your money manifesting will stop working. You'll be cosmically constipated. Whatever you are thinking, dreaming or doing is what you are going to get back ten-fold.

Because I'm such an awesome manifester now, I have to be extra careful about my thoughts, because I can manifest instantly when I'm in the zone. That kind of power can be used for good or bad, it's a double edged sword. Luckily, you can learn to make positivity your default mood, so you manifest good stuff instead of more drama.

This doesn't mean you become a Pollyanna or a robot who isn't allowed to feel bad occasionally. You're allowed to have PMS. You're allowed to have an off-day as long as you pick yourself up and get straight back on the lucky bitch train as soon as possible.

I'm just a normal person, I like to moan at my husband sometimes, I love reading columnist *Lainey Gossip* for the latest Hollywood goss and sometimes I have a bad day and just want to wallow in misery. But it doesn't last long because I know my income will be affected if I don't snap out of it quickly.

You Are Richer Than You Think

There is more abundance in your life than you even know. In fact, you're probably ignoring money all over the place. I know there are thousands of unclaimed dollars around me and I bet you a hundred bucks you have heaps too.

Just now, I have a travel insurance claim I'm sitting on, health rebates I haven't gotten around to, potential clients waiting for a follow up and bank accounts I keep forgetting to close.

It doesn't even have to be large amounts of money. You could be ignoring money right in front of you.

For example, I had this friend who had coins all over her house. She didn't even notice but there was money strewn all over the floor, in glasses, between couch cushions and on top of the fridge. What message does that say about how she values money?

Mark and I have this gorgeous mosaic bowl full of money. Whenever we find spare coins, we put them in this bowl and it looks beautiful. At first I thought, "What if people just help themselves?". It kind of freaked me out to display that money so openly, but then I saw a box of coins on the counter of my local store. A sign said *"if you need one, take it. If you have a spare one, leave it"*. I thought that was so beautiful, so if you're at my house and you need some coins, take them. If you have spare hanging around, chuck them in!

Before you start to send out messages to the Universe saying "I want $10,000 or $100,000 to show up", acknowledge all the money, and things of value you already have in your life. That way you are saying to the Universe *"Thanks for all this, and I'm ready for even <u>more</u>"*, you're making room for it and proving you're truly prepared.

I recently found $1 on the floor at the gym. I looked around and for a second I thought, "I can't pick this up, what will people think of me?". Then I remembered what I'd tell my fellow lucky bitches and I picked it up and said "thanks Universe!"

The Quickest Way to Feel Rich Now

Gratitude is the single greatest way to change your state from a feeling of poverty or lack, into feeling rich.

Mark and I always acknowledge every lucky thing that happens to us, even if it's a parking spot outside the shops, we'll say out loud "Look at that, just for us, how lucky are we?"

Tracking your income is a great start and then when you shift how you feel about it, you'll see amazing things happen. You'll attract more!

You might see that you've "only" manifested money

on two days out of five. When you send gratitude to that experience, rather than blaming yourself, you're giving permission to the Universe to send you *more.* Say to yourself "Omg, you clever lucky bitch! That's awesome; I can't wait to see what you do next week!"

"Got no diamonds, got no pearls.
Still, I think I'm a lucky girl – I've got the sun in the mornin' and the moon at night."
Irving Berlin, *Annie Get Your Gun*

In Access Consciousness, the magic question is *"How can it get any better than this?"*, not in a resigned or spoilt way, but actually with excitement and anticipation. Seriously, how can it get *even* better?

Before I go to sleep, I love listing out things I'm grateful for, it sends me off to sleep in a feeling of abundance and wealth.

Where's YOUR hidden wealth that you're not even acknowledging?

When I first searched around for unclaimed money in my life, I realised that I had money accounts all over the place. I had superannuation accounts I had completely forgotten about. I also realised I had been holding myself back from claiming money from my US book sales because I was procrastinating over getting my US tax number. It was going to cost me a couple of hundred dollars to get the tax sorted out, but the sales income was just sitting there waiting for me to claim! I had uncashed cheques sitting in my wallet. I had unclaimed insurance forms. I had clients who owed me money. All of this unclaimed and unacknowledged abundance, sitting around waiting for me.

Action – go on a treasure hunt!

Do you have more than one bank account with money sitting in it? You probably have a million unused gift vouchers (that's pretty much like cash). If you have accrued leave entitlements at work calculate the dollar value of that. Maybe some of your belongings, your assets, have increased in value, like your house, the value of your jewellery or random collectables. Go and collect all the money that is scattered through your car, clothes, home, and work desk. Trust me you'll find a lot.

You might find a whole bunch of expired gift vouchers and pamper certificates (BOO!), but you'll learn next time, gorgeous. On my last round of Money Bootcamp, here are some of the things my participants found:

- *Unclaimed tax rebate of $90*
- *Reminder on a Post-It to remortgage house (saved $120/month)*
- *Costco refund of $120*
- *A hair voucher worth $180*
- *Over $13,000 of forgotten loans to family members*
- *Loyalty card with free coffee ready to be claimed worth $3.50*
- *Enough frequent flyer points for a free flight*
- *$300 hidden in an old book (seriously!)*
- *Unclaimed scratch cards and lottery tickets*
- *Coins from old handbags $83.45*
- *Foreign currency in old travel wallets $100*

- *Fraud claim form for bank refund for $100*
- *A book of forgotten stamps worth $25*
- *A forgotten and unclaimed rental security deposit of $1000*
- *Amazon credit of $15*
- *Forgotten PayPal money $53*
- *Uncashed cheques/checks from clients $850*

You are literally surrounded with money that's just sitting there and it's like the Universe is saying, "We've given it to you! Use it!"

It's so important to acknowledge and actually use every bit of cash and value that comes into your life. Here's why - just imagine that you have a goal of manifesting $5000 every month. You're getting frustrated because you're only hitting $3000. So, you're like *"Dude, where's my money?"*. You start thinking that this Law of Attraction crap doesn't work for you, that you're a bad person and you're going to die a lonely, broke old maid.

But the Universe IS giving it to you, if you pay close attention. Round up all those hidden opportunities, I bet you've hit your goal every time.

Automate Your Positive Feelings

I'm the laziest person in the world. Things have to be really easy for me to stick. I rarely remember to take vitamins, going to the gym is a drag for me and I always, always try and find the short-cut.

In my book *Lucky Bitch,* I shared that in my first telemarketing job, I refused to actually telemarket. I made fewer than 10 cold calls the two months I worked there.

Yet, I was number two salesperson in the company. How did that happen?

I got bored making calls and the odds were so low of actually making a sale, it was the world's most demotivating job, so one night I tried an experiment. When everyone else went to the pub at 9pm, I'd stay and see how many potential customers called in wanting to sign up. Turns out, a lot. Enough to make me number two sales person. Yes, I had to work an extra hour for free but the commissions made up for it. Plus, I didn't have to do the painful work of making cold calls.

So, I'm big fan of finding easy short-cuts for the Law of Attraction to work for you. One extremely easy and automatic way is to build your desires into your everyday environment. This is my single greatest manifestation tip because you don't have to think about it, there's absolutely no will power or effort required.

What are your passwords for your computer, your phone, your online banking? Are they something completely random, or do they excite you every time you type them in? This is something you do anyway, each and every day, at least 10 times, so make them something like '6figures' which was my laptop password for a year until I hit it. Now it's '7figures'!

I've just changed my online banking password to be my income goal for next year. I already achieved last year's one, so it's time to update it.

What are you choosing for your bank account names? Some banks allow you to change the name of your account. So you could have 'savings account' or 'savings for house' but you can change it to be anything. Rather than having one called "Debt" account, name it "You Can

Be Financially Free' account or 'Hawaii Holiday".

My savings account is called "Money Loves Me". Every time I put money in there, I'm reminded of my mantra, "Money loves me and takes care of me". My expenses and receipts folder in my Gmail is also called "Money Loves Me". Who knows how often I actually see it, but it's there casting a subtle subliminal spell. Every little bit helps.

Set up automatic reminders on your phone with pop up messages, (on the iPhone, you do it under your calendar and set it as a recurring reminder). Mine currently say "congratulations on selling a million copies. You are a publishing success story!" and "have fun driving your new silver Lexus Hybrid".

Yours can say "remember, you are beautiful!" or "way to go on breaking six figures this year!". They'll pop up out of the blue, so when it happens, take a second or two out of your day to think, "Hell yeah!".

You can go crazy with these little messages, so they are infusing your conscious and subconscious mind every single day. You literally can't go an hour without at least a small reminder of your goals. It will make a huge difference.

Here are some of my best lazy manifesting tips:

- Listen to subliminal CDs with messages about abundance and wealth as you work;
- Put Post-Its around the house with your goals written on them in present tense;
- Read or listen to autobiographies of wealthy women on your commute;
- Display your dream board where you can see it

(printed out, on your computer desktop and on your phone);

- Doodle pictures of your goals when you're on the phone, or gaze at your dream board when you're on hold;
- Listen to motivational CDs in your car so as soon as you turn on the ignition, you're immediately back in the zone;
- Laminate a goal list for your shower;
- Write your biggest goal in the shower steam each morning. I draw hearts and dollar signs every day;
- Put your goal list on the back of the toilet door, may as well use that time well!
- Keep a notebook in your purse so you can re-write your Be, Do & Have list when you're in a waiting room;
- Sign up for Notes from the Universe at Tut.com;
- Get my weekly newsletter at www.LuckyBitch.com;
- Use novelty money items like napkins printed like dollar bills;
- Keep $100 in your wallet and never spend it. Just looking at it daily will make you feel abundant;
- Put a tiny goal list in the window portion of your wallet where you'd normally put your license;
- Get a personalised number plate - mine says LUCKYB;
- Make a money related playlist on iTunes;
- Watch shows about money and rich people;
- Set up at automatic savings account, so you have a rainy day fund.

One of my favourite secret success tools is subliminal learning affirmations. I use them for everything; creativity, relaxation, self-love *and* abundance. Subliminal means "below the threshold" which means that the messages are just below your conscious perception. It can activate specific regions of the brain without you being consciously aware of it, but the message is still heard by your unconscious mind.

Affirmations work beautifully but you're not going to sit there for hours repeating them to yourself. Who has the time or the will-power? No, hearing them recorded with beautiful music over the top is an excellent (and lazy) alternative that's much more practical for the average person.

Listening to subliminal meditation tapes has definitely worked for me and I think it's worth trying. Some people say that works entirely because of a placebo effect, mainly because you *believe* it will work, but that's fine by me. Remember, throw everything at it.

Participants on my Lucky Bitch Money Bootcamp get my special Money Mantras subliminal meditation as a free bonus and even I was astounded at how well it worked!

I recorded 1111 mantras and affirmations about money, then put a soundtrack of relaxing beach sounds over the top. You can't actually hear the affirmations consciously (unless you listen really really hard) but the message goes into your subconscious in a powerful way. You can just play it in the background of whatever you're doing, even when you're asleep (just not while operating heavy machinery). No effort required.

Within a few days of sending it out to my Bootcamp peeps, I started to get all these random emails about crazy money manifestations.

The point is - *everything helps.* If you want a free 5 minute version of the money mantras subliminal CD, you can claim yours at www.GetRichLuckyBitch.com using password MONEYLOVE to access.

Will Your Goals into Existence

When I was in the process of writing my first book, *Lucky Bitch,* I still wasn't confident in myself as an author, so I changed my email signature to, *"Denise Duffield-Thomas – Coach and Author"*.

This might not seem like a big deal, but for me, I didn't yet believe I was a coach or an author. I felt like I was pretending by changing my signature. But as I wrote my book, I saw that signature every day and it reminded me that I was definitely in the process of becoming an author, even though I had trouble telling people about it.

Even though I had done my coach training, I wasn't ready to claim being a coach either, so it was difficult for me to make money from it. It was a tiny little thing but I saw that signature multiple times every day and it gave me confidence. Other people saw it and they believed I was both of those things. Their belief strengthened my own, which *willed* it into reality.

After a few weeks, I changed the signature to *"Author of Lucky Bitch"* and it gave me confidence to finish my book. It helped me step into an energetic space where I *was* that person. Every time I saw it, I believed in myself just a tiny bit more.

The same is true for when you create account names when you join an online forum or Twitter. Be aware of the energy you're putting out there. It's a bit of a pet hate of mine when people don't put their name on their account and instead they use a nickname. My client Kris Emery used "sohighlystrung" as her Twitter name but has since changed it to her business name. Much better energy, right?

Seriously, Denise does all this stuff really make a difference? Aren't you going a bit overboard?

No. Words have power. Everything has significance. Every action you take has significance to your self-worth and inevitably your net-worth. All these things might seem random, but it all compounds over time to increase your wealth consciousness.

So next time you're online, change your signature, your passwords, your names of all your accounts to ensure they are exactly what you want them to be, not something random and without meaning. Really look and see what you are putting out there to the Universe.

These things are easy changes to make and require very little thought or effort on your behalf. It's the lazy girl's guide to manifesting!

Every time you see one of your automatic actions or type it your goal instead of a password, it's another message to your subconscious that you are ready for your goals to manifest, that you are ready to claim being a wealthy woman.

Crowd Out the Negativity

My VIP client, Jess Nazarali, gets her health clients to simply crowd out bad food with healthier options instead of making massive changes and ending up sabotaging their diets. It's the easiest way to make behaviour change, otherwise it feels too hard.

All of these easy actions compound over time and the idea is that all the positive messages about money will crowd out the negative. It's really the lazy person's manifesting tool bag. Look out for my next book, *Lazy Bitch*, if I can ever get around to writing it!

Be aware of the energy you put out on social media, the words and phrases you use, and for Goddess sake, please don't spread urban myths and fear-based messages, they create fear for everyone and are a complete waste of time and energy. Only spread positive messages.

When I'm having a bad day, I stay away from social media. I'm aware of my growing audience and I wouldn't want to infect anyone with my (temporary) negativity. Sure, I'll share real life struggles to show that I'm not perfect either but I see my job as inspiring people, not being a Denise Downer. Besides, if I share it, I'll stay in that state longer and I want to get out as quickly as possible.

You'll never hear me say things like "It's so hard to get clients/make money/get out of debt", or use language like *desperate, broke, scared*, etc.

I don't complain about taxes, the government or the price of things. I rarely go on negative based rants (occasionally something weird and Virgo related, like how nobody knows how to properly hang clothes for optimal drying time – that's just *wrong*) because it will infect my day too.

If I see too many negative messages from a friend, client or family member, I'll hide them from my news feed. I choose the news I want to watch and avoid most forms of sensationalist media (except for my Lainey Gossip addiction). I don't watch much horror anymore (except The Walking Dead) and side-step any political or religious discussions that might raise my blood pressure. It's not worth it.

I've phased out friendships with people who invite too much drama in their life or use more negative than positive language or obsess about their problems without doing anything about it.

Honestly, it's okay to say no and ban people from your life who aren't adding to it in a positive way.

Basically, YOU CAN CHOOSE. You choose the messages you take into your brain.

I'd say more on this topic, but my friend and mentor Leonie Dawson says it better and I'm quoting a paragraph from her book, *73 Lessons Every Goddess Must Know*:

You Have Permission

by Leonie Dawson

Dearest Goddess,

Today, and every day, you have permission.

You have permission.

Today, and every day, you have permission.

You have permission to say no to demands on your time that don't light you up, and don't give energy back to you.

You have permission to not give a crap what's happening outside your world, and keep your energy focussed on what you are creating.

You have permission to let go of friendships that make you feel like shit.

You have permission to say no whenever you like, however you like, in whatever kind of voice you like, without feeling like only Mean Girls Say No and Nice Girls Say Yes. That's bull. Yes and No have equal weighting - what's important is if you use them when they are the best thing for you, not out of fear, obligation or guilt.

You have permission to know that Yes is powerful, and so is No. The power comes from you using either from your highest spirit and truest integrity.

You have permission to change. You have permission to not be the person you once were.

You have permission to get angry and self-righteous, and to also glean the wisdom from those emotions. They are leading you to where your boundaries are, and where they have been crossed, and what you need to do from now on.

You have permission to be exactly how you are.

You have permission to not be more like anyone else in the world, even if you think they are better, wiser or more popular. You have permission to be more like yourself, your gifts and your wisdom.

You have permission to not care what other people think of you.

You have permission to not try to change what other people think of you. You can't ever argue that you are a good person. They will either know you are, or not. You don't need to spend time with people who don't believe in you.

You have permission to do things that your friends and family do not.

You have permission to be wild, expressive, truthful, exciting and outspoken.

You have permission to not accept friendship requests on Facebook, or anywhere else in your life. You have permission to block people whenever you like.

You have permission to share as much or as little as you like. You have permission to blog, or not blog. You have permission to Twitter, or not to Twitter. It doesn't really matter. As long as it's making you happy, that's the best thing.

You have permission to suck at a wide variety of activities. It's okay. You make up for it with your million other brilliance particles.

You have permission to be whatever body shape you like.

You have permission to choose, and choose again. And then choose again.

You have permission to not always be a perfect image of something.

You have permission to be a contradiction.

You have permission to not go to your school reunion, unless it really excites you and delights you, and you would love to really heart-reconnect with people you went to school with.

You have permission to not be interested in the newest fad: harem pants, geek glasses, Polaroid cameras, scrapbooking, macramé. You also have permission to be totally obsessed with them, if it makes your heart light up.

You have permission to cut people from your life. You have permission to surround yourself with people who are good and loving and nurturing to you.

You have permission to be a disappointment to some people, as long as you're not a disappointment to yourself.

You have permission to do nothing whenever you like.

You have permission to make your big dream come true.

You have permission to not do it all perfectly, or have all your shit together.

You have permission to not forgive people. You have permission to forgive people when it's right for you.

You have permission to think some people are crazy. You have permission to think some people are smigging ice-cream with chocolate and wafers and sprinkles and cherries on top.

You have permission to not have the perfect relationship.

You have permission to not have a relationship.

You have permission to take whatever time you need for you.

You have permission to make ridiculous choices for yourself.

You have permission to use and listen to your intuition. To feel when things are off, and to remove yourself from them, even when you don't quite know why. You will always find out why. Our intuition is here to serve us.

You have permission to be down. You have permission to be up.

You have permission to still believe in unicorns and fairies.

You have permission to believe in things that other people think are very very odd and strange. You have permission to not care. You have permission to believe in things that make your life wholer, richer and deeper. You have permission to make your own world that is the truest painting of you.

You have permission to suck at colouring in.

You have permission to say bugger off to anyone who has ever told you that you're not good enough, you're not worth it, you are not beautiful, you are not lovable and you are not the most divine, wise, delicious Goddess to walk the planet.

You have permission to know that you are.

You have permission to swear when you like, however you like, to your reckless abandon.

You have permission to not be the best of anything – just the best of yourself. And some days, just the best you can do that day.

You have permission to not always give. You have permission to fill your own cup up first.

You have permission to have things around you that delight you.

You have permission to live in a tipi if you want to, or a mansion. Whatever makes your spirit shine is the right thing for you.

You have permission to make choices on whether it makes your spirit shine.

You have permission to know you are a goddess, even when it doesn't feel like it. Even when you feel utterly human. Even when you want nothing more than to climb under your blanket, or light up the sky.

You are a goddess.
You have permission.
You have permission.
You have permission.

big love,
Leonie.

* * *

You can find the gorgeous Leonie at
www.LeonieDawson.com

Chapter Summary

- You are richer than you think
- Gratitude is the quickest way to feel rich now and when you feel rich, you'll attract more money.
- Money is all around you, open up your eyes and go on a treasure hunt

Bonus - get your free subliminal money meditation from www.GetRichLuckyBitch.com using password LOVEMONEY.

$

Upgrade Your Life Now

"Little changes and little choices add up to be revolutionary changes in your life."
Sarah Ban Breathnach

I believe in making quantum jumps in success, but sometimes moving forward even a tiny bit will help, especially when you're feeling blocked around money. Here's what I hear from women all the time:

"I can't wait until I'm rich"

And they talk about all the things they will buy "when" they're rich.

Mark and I used to have that conversation *all the time* thinking that we were acting "as if" we were going to be rich. In reality, we were pushing it further away to "one day". It was exactly like when we were dating. Friends and family would ask us when we were getting married and Mark would answer "in two or three years". Finally I told him "Buddy, you know that has to start counting down, right? It has to be two years, then one year and then eventually you have to actually produce a ring".

You can't be rich *one day*. You have to start to-day. Yes, it's a hella fun to speculate about the future, but do you know what's even *fun-ner*? Actually *living* it.

You can't rely on someone else to make you rich. I know, I tried. I thought that Mark would be the stable breadwinner and my money would come "someday". It didn't.

When we were first dating, I earned more than him (he was a student), but then he started out-earning me at work while I got overlooked for promotions and pay increases. It sucked at first, because I was the one reading all the money books, going to wealth development seminars and investing in coaching. It wasn't until I worked on my money mindset in the *real world* and upgraded my life before anyone else gave it to me, that's when my income took off.

I keep on talking about the "real world", as opposed to the one in our heads. It's so easy to live in a state of "what if" when you're reading inspiring wealth books and we can all imagine what we'd do with a million bucks without much trouble, but ask us to pay for an upgrade before we feel "ready" - no way!

When you live a life of constant but incremental upgrade, you *will* attract more money into your life. Teeny tiny amounts at first and then more and more. The speed and amount of money totally depends on your bravery and willingness to push yourself further.

"Life shrinks or expands in proportion
to one's courage."
Anaïs Nin

Now – I'm not talking about going into credit card debt or spending money you don't have. Spending money just to impress other people also doesn't work. If overspending is your sabotage pattern, spending more isn't going to fix anything. It's not going to work to buy what Robert Kiyosaki calls "doodads", unless it makes you feel really good about yourself.

Debbie had a problem with spending money. In her own words she would "spend money like an alcoholic would drink". She would do it in secret and then feel awful about it later. She was addicted to spending, but not on things of value that improved her life, she was spending for the sake of spending, a classic sabotage.

To stop this sabotaging behaviour, Deb made the decision that their bank account was never going to go to zero. She created a new "energetic overdraft limit" that was just a few hundred dollars to start with. As long as she had a positive bank balance, she slowly weaned herself off the urge to spend until there was nothing left. Then, over time, she slowly increased that amount, until she was comfortable having several thousand in her account and created a new energetic comfort level.

You don't always have to spend a lot of money to feel rich. In fact, at the time of writing this book, I don't have a credit card (this is about to change so I can maximise Frequent Flyer points). Since I moved back to Australia recently and I work for myself, I couldn't be bothered doing the additional paperwork to get a credit card, so I experienced the pleasure of paying things with cash. I paid for my laser eye surgery in cash (literally fifty one hundred dollar bills). You bet that made me feel rich. I bought my car in cash (again, literally) and owning that car outright felt amazing at the time.

But there were many little things over the last few years that also made me feel rich. When I felt rich, I acted rich and then had the courage to change more things in my life. A beautiful virtuous cycle.

In this chapter, you'll be inspired to put your money in places that might make you feel uncomfortable and your comfort level will be completely personal to you. You might be totally okay with spending money on organic food, but you wear the skankiest underwear known to womankind. You might be totally comfortable staying in 5-star hotels but the thought of saving even the tiniest amount of money each month scares the shit out of you. It's okay. It doesn't matter what your particular money "problem" or sabotage is, the way we solve that is by making tiny upgrades.

It might seem crazy at first to be spending money on yourself or by living more extravagantly than you're used to, but by making minor upgrades you will to start to vibrate at a higher frequency of wealth because you will feel the joy and satisfaction of having or doing those things *in the real world.* And guess what? Yes – you guessed it – you will attract more positive vibrations and your money manifesting will become easier and more powerful.

Let's change the conversation from "I can't wait" to "I'm so lucky" and "this is so much fun". We'll upgrade your life in such clever, sneaky ways that your favourite forms of sabotage won't even have a chance. Yes, you might have momentary freak-outs, but you have the tools to deal with it. It just becomes a fun game – what can you upgrade in your life next?

When you start making minor upgrades to your life,

you essentially build and grow the power of your manifesting muscle.

The Law of Incremental Upgrade

I coined this concept because I was fed up with my constant backsliding after the hype wore off from another money book or personal development seminar. I was initially excited but I had no idea what to *do* with the information - everything seemed so overwhelming. I wanted to live in a beautiful beach mansion by the sea, have an amazing car, wear gorgeous clothes (that actually *fit* properly and didn't smell of a charity shop), have nice hair and be surrounded by wealth, ease and beauty. I wanted to make a teleporting leap out of my current life into something amazing and have everything change in an instant.

Instead, I looked around at the *reality* of my life; the small flat that was literally the only area we could afford, full of newly arrived immigrants who left as quickly as they could and the house itself that was so wonkily built that all the furniture slanted in different directions. Everything in my life was make-do. I had so many workarounds to make it through the day. You know when you don't even realize what you're putting up with, until you have someone come to stay and you say, "Oh, the shower works if you jiggle it a bit and then crank the handle five times". Virtually everything in my life was like that. I remember our cheap Ikea bed broke and I spend a whole Saturday constructing this elaborate fix out of ply-wood and glue because we couldn't afford to buy a new one.

Everything in my life was cheap, cheap, cheap, but I felt paralysed to do anything about it. I didn't have the money to fix everything. There was *too much crap* to handle all at once and I put pressure on myself to suddenly become this rich chick overnight. But even if I got a windfall or pay increase, nothing really changed and the money left quickly. I wasn't energetically *aligned* to wealth because my overwhelming experience was mediocrity and a "make-do" mindset.

Let me be clear here - the way I experienced poverty in that time of my life wasn't poverty as we know it on a global scale. I understand that. My "shitty" life and wonky flat was someone else's idea of extreme wealth. I don't think it's fair that people starve or die from needless diseases and I'm not being insensitive to that. However this isn't a book about global economic justice (that is an incredibly important topic but not my area of expertise). This is a book about removing all obstacles from you being as wealthy as you want to be.

The ironic thing is that when you commit only to making incremental upgrades you actually can make the quantum leaps much quicker. This simple process has changed my life, increased my income and *finally* allowed to me to feel rich.

Create Your Upgrade Plan

Begin by revisiting your Be, Do & Have list and add anything you'd have if your life was truly First Class. This kind of thinking is harder than it sounds.

This is not about having a gold-plated car (unless that's your goal, in which case, I might judge you!). This is not about owning your own private jet if you don't want one. This isn't about the most conspicuous consumption you can imagine. I'm just asking you to add what you'd like in your life if money wasn't an issue. If you had the choice, *what would you choose*?

Sometimes the upgrade is actually a downgrade. It's about making your life simpler, more pleasurable and less stressful. It's also much more real. You might not see yourself as someone who wants a private jet, but what class would you like to fly? Premium economy to start with?

There is no right or wrong answer. Your idea of First Class might evolve over time. It might get more extravagant, it might actually get simpler.

When you have a juicy list of First Class items, make a list of everything in your life that's the complete opposite of this list. Anything that annoys you, embarrasses you, makes you feel poor or is more like Economy Class.

Then, you simply pick *one thing* at a time and upgrade it to the very next level. Just a teeny tiny bit, so you don't freak out.

Say your *idea* of First Class underwear is La Perla but in *reality* you're wearing five year old granny pants from Target. You will probably freak out if I told you to get your dingy covered ass to La Perla and splash out a couple of hundred bucks on a set of frilly lingerie.

It would feel too scary or frivolous. It could cause you to spiral into your own personal brand of sabotage (more on that in the next chapter) and you'd probably regret spending the money. Plus it's only one pair of undies, so you'd still have to keep your skanky panties for the days your special new pants are getting washed. It won't make that much of a noticeable difference in your life.

Instead of making a massive leap that you don't feel ready for, go for a tiny upgrade. Choose the next best upgrade from Target. Maybe you upgrade to pretty sets from a mid-priced store and work your way up to the fanciest underwear. But wearing even *slightly* nicer panties will make you feel richer. I did this with my lululemon workout clothes. I threw out some of my skanky tights and worn out sports bras and just bought a couple of pieces. Every time I could afford to buy more, I threw out the old ones. Working out just felt more abundant in lululemon and I felt like a rich person. Soon it was an easy decision to only buy quality workout wear because I deserved it. Now I wear lululemon every day, it's my unofficial work uniform.

Now, nice undies might be easy for you, so don't choose that as your first upgrade. Pick something that really does bug you and makes you feel poor. It could be old makeup, scrappy towels full of holes, a broken chair in your kitchen, bad lighting in your bathroom, dirty windows in your office or something else.

You choose what you'll upgrade first and start from the bottom of the barrel and improve it as incrementally as you can handle right now.

Each time you upgrade something small, it becomes part of *who you are* and crowds out your old poverty story. You're sending a clear message to the Universe that you are worth nice things.

Your new way of being becomes your minimum standard and have you noticed that you always find money for things you value? The good feelings this gives you on a daily basis compound over time and the Universe provides the money for each upgrade. As you continue to track your incoming money, you'll start to see that the Universe rewards you for feeling richer with actual *cash*. It always happens. When you start off incrementally, you'll get the urge to make bigger and better leaps as you feel braver and better about yourself.

You don't even need to spend that much money to feel richer. Sometimes the difference between the cheapest option and the next best is only a few bucks, especially for consumer goods like coffee or tea, hand-soap, chocolate, hummus or stockings. Your basic bar of cheap chocolate is a few dollars and the fancy version could be double that but in the grand scheme of things, it's still a cheap luxury that will make you feel richer and you'll probably eat less of it!

Remember when you started digging out all those gift vouchers, collecting all that random money and generally cashing in? Well, it's time to do something with it.

If you've been putting off booking hair appointments, massage appointments, facials, anything, now is the time to do it. Start getting those appointments in your diary and use the extra money that was just sitting there waiting for the taking. Because it was found treasure, spend at least a portion of it guilt-free!

You can also donate your unwanted gift vouchers to others for an instant feel good fix. Pay it forward and practice what it feels like to be a generously wealthy woman.

It's not even the stingy money habits you need to give up, it's the *perception of yourself* that you have to break. That you're not the "kind of person" who chooses the fancy option, stays in the nice hotel or gets a cab instead of the bus.

Nobody is going to give you permission to be a wealthy woman. You have to create it by *feeling* it in increasingly small ways on a day to day basis. It's not enough to meditate or visualise being rich (although that's useful), you've got to put yourself in it and feel it in the real world. You prove it to yourself by the small daily actions you take.

"What you believe has more power than what you dream or wish or hope for. You become what you believe."
Oprah

If you really can't bring yourself to spend more money or things feel tight, you can start by wearing your favourite clothes more often (they might actually be the only things left in your wardrobe after all that decluttering), wear your most awesome shoes, use all the beauty products in the bottom draw, use your perfume every day and give yourself some extra minutes to do your hair and makeup. It's free but you'll feel amazing.

Allow yourself to use your best bed linen more often, or better yet, go out and buy gorgeous Egyptian cotton linen and make your bed a real oasis of calmness and a special place to rest your head. You will go to bed feeling richer and wake up feeling richer. Imagine what you can achieve with that kind of confidence?

Lastly, you commit to taking everything to the next level, but not all at once. Again, just pick one or two symbolic things to work on each week and see how it feels.

If you usually park miles away from your meeting, practice getting valet parking. That thirty bucks will teach you more about your money fears than reading fifty money books will. It puts your new money beliefs to the test.

If you're a fast food addict, break your habit and

upgrade the quality of your food. If you're already a whiz in the kitchen, take it to the next level and start buying better ingredients. Imagine the pleasure that cooking with real vanilla beans or fancy spices will give you.

You could upgrade your beauty regime, by going to the salon more frequently than you're used to. Maybe you wait until your dark (or grey) roots are practically down around your ears before you make an appointment, so go more regularly. Say yes to the extra hydration treatment. Get a blow dry just for the hell of it.

I don't know about you but when I get a good blow dry, I feel like a million bucks. The day feels sunnier, everyone smiles at me and I'm practically bouncing down the street with my own personal wind machine, Beyoncé style. That's the best fifty bucks you can spend to improve your money mindset.

When I have a speaking engagement or a conference to attend, I'll always get my hair professionally blow-dried. You know how much time that saves me when I'm travelling? It's amazing and it has a knock on effect. It's a small price that I'm willing to pay for the luxurious feeling it gives me.

Looking and feeling great can have a direct impact on your earning potential. Women who are well groomed earn more, it's a fact. You will attract better clients when you feel confident. Spending that money before it shows up is an awesome investment.

Make a Highly Symbolic Upgrade

To really show the Universe you are serious about wanting more money in your life, you need to show how much *you* value money with highly symbolic upgrades.

One example for me was when I decided to get a book keeper. I had been putting it off because I thought it was going to be expensive and I felt like I shouldn't spend money on something like that.

What I realised was, if I wanted money to be a top priority in my life and in my business, I needed to be organised with my money. I was neglecting my book-keeping, and I hadn't done my taxes on time, so I had to pay a fine. Looking at my receipts piling up made me want to vomit.

I had to find a symbolic upgrade that really told money, "Hey, you're a priority in my life", and showed the Universe I was serious about going pro in my business.

I knew I had to hire a book keeper but I just really didn't want to spend the money on it. I worried about where I would get that extra money from, but every time I thought about my taxes or looked at my receipts piling up, it made me feel so sick. It was hugely wasted energy and I knew that this was a symbolic upgrade for my business and my money, so I decided to stop expending extra energy on worrying about doing my taxes and I finally hired a great book keeper and it's been the best investment ever!

What do you need to upgrade in your business to go pro this year?

Think about what symbolic actions you can take that will show that you highly value money in your life.

Maybe if you have a business, you could start a business bank account, or get a better credit card that gives you reward points. You could get a separate business credit card. You could even just pay your bills on time or early by setting up direct debits that go easily out of your account. What are some of the things that you're going to do now that really show money, "Hey, you and me, we're friends".

Think about how it would feel if you prioritised money in your life, if you made wealth or affluence an absolute top priority in your life?

What would a millionaire choose?

Sarah on my Bootcamp was going through a divorce and had to find a new place to live. She had looked at a variety of apartments, some cheap, some more expensive. She fell in love with a more expensive apartment and decided to take that one because it was what she really wanted.

Sarah said: "At first, I was not exactly sure how I was going to pay for my new lifestyle now I was divorced, but I remembered the lessons that Denise taught me, and after I made the commitment, things just kind of fell into place to make it happen".

Sarah had agonised over the decision on whether to take the more expensive apartment. She even had people say to her that she should get the cheaper apartment because it was the *sensible* thing to do (don't you hate that!)

For Sarah, going for the more expensive place was symbolic of how she wanted her new life to be. She didn't want to just settle for the cheaper option.

"There was a kind of feeling of, 'Yes, that's the smart choice. That's the one that rationally I should probably go for because I would save some money.' But I'd be in the same place and kind of in the same part of my life. It wouldn't really signify anything was different. Whereas the new apartment totally signifies that my life is different," Sarah said.

When you are faced with a choice like this where you have to decide whether to stay small and cheap or go big, bold and expensive, try and think what would the millionaire version of yourself choose? Would you move into a one bedroom condo or the condo with two bedrooms and a study so you can have a proper office and space to do your work? That way with the extra space you can show the Universe that you value your ability to be able to make money.

You might be like Sarah and start to think, "I shouldn't want that". It's like at some point we've been told you shouldn't want to have the best. You shouldn't want more. You should just be happy with what you've got. Well this whole book is about giving yourself permission to not only want better for yourself, but to upgrade your life in all the ways that are going to make it possible for your dreams to come true, no matter what they are.

This is not about being ostentatious or becoming a person you do not want to be. This is about embracing your power and making your life better, enhancing who you are through money.

Practice Being Generous

A lot of women have a dream of becoming wealthy so they can give money away, a worthy ideal for sure. Some personal development and abundance teachers say you should tithe 10% of your income to charities, your church or anywhere else you get spiritual food. I think that's a beautiful practice, but again, don't get caught up in thinking that's the only way to get rich.

I love giving when I feel called to and this past year, I made several large donations that pushed me right out of my comfort zone, literally I was sweating and feeling sick about it, but it also felt big and abundant and exactly in line with my vision of myself as a rich woman who is moved by something and gets out her cheque-book to help. It wasn't easy but I had to step into that vision of myself and put up some cash.

So, if giving is important to you, start giving *now* in a way that makes you feel generous and happy. If you give money to a homeless guy out of guilt, then practice making a big contribution to a talented busker instead and see how it feels. Read the paper and when you see an inspiring story, send some money. It will feel much better than a regular direct debit to a charity that you never think about again.

Donate money to Kiva.org each month and see your contributions build up over time.

Tip just a bit more than you're comfortable with and practice feeling generous. That nervous feeling is good – it's training yourself to be more abundant *now*, not when you're richer tomorrow.

> *"The secret to living the life of your dreams is to start living the life of your dreams today, in every little way you possibly can."*
> Mike Dooley

Making all these relatively minor upgrades will show the Universe that you are ready for more and you really believe you deserve it. After a while all the minor upgrading will add up to big leaps towards your ultimate goals. You don't have to go on a crazy shopping spree. Just start with one thing at a time until it becomes part of your normal routine and you feel confident you can always afford it. Then pick something else.

"Whoever said money can't buy happiness didn't know where to shop."
Gertrude Stein

Live Like a Wealthy Person Now

Mark and I are really busy people and to be honest, cleaning is not our favourite thing to do. So years ago, even before we earned good money, we had a cleaner once a fortnight. We always knew that when we were rich "one day", we'd have a cleaner, but one day we decided to try it out and get one way before we could actually afford it.

That year, Mark and I decided that instead of giving each other expensive Christmas presents, we'd have a strict budget of $10 each. Yet we had a cleaner and I spent money on personal development conferences and a coach. We decided that even though getting our cleaner felt like a big deal at the time, it was worth it because it made us feel rich in a way that presents didn't.

We were willing to sacrifice things we didn't care about in order to make an upgrade that would make us feel richer. We freed up time and energy to work on our careers and make even more money, so we always found the money *and* it paid off.

So when we moved into our penthouse, we upgraded

to a weekly cleaner and the Universe tested our boundaries again. We interviewed some cleaners who didn't want to make beds or wash dishes or take out the garbage. I found myself thinking *"I don't want to be bossy and ask them to do things they don't want to do"*. I finally realised what I was doing, I was being freaking ridiculous. I decided to take back my power and was really clear and upfront with what I wanted. I was just like *"this is what I want. How much is it going to cost for me to get it the way I want?"*

And you know what happened next, we found a great cleaner that did everything we asked for. By being upfront and not being afraid to use my power and not worry if they thought I was a bitch, I ended up finding the perfect person.

When we have kids, I'll upgrade again to having a cleaner a few times a week and add other household chores into the mix. My ultimate dream is to have a full time housekeeper who makes me lunch and does all the house chores and our weekly errands. Each upgrade gets me closer to the goal, gives me practice in managing someone and avoids the sudden shock of hiring a full time person.

Start today by imagining the life you want in the future and taking one practice step towards it.

Get Ready For the Money

I told you how I manifested our penthouse, but how did I get ready for that with incremental upgrades? It didn't just happen overnight and I didn't move house every six months to slightly bigger and better ones. This one was actually a big leap in reality and because I didn't want to move every six months, I had to upgrade my belief incrementally that it was actually even possible.

So I spent every weekend looking at beautiful houses on the internet and when I felt braver, I went to auctions and open house days for increasingly expensive houses just to experience my ideal lifestyle even just for a few minutes.

Walking through these gorgeous homes I affirmed "Yes, I do really want this for myself". Every time I walked into those stunning homes, I pictured myself living there, and I'd whisper to myself "*Universe, this is what I want*". My goal was cemented in the top of my mind whenever I visited these dream homes. I could see it, smell it, hear it, and, most importantly, *feel it*.

Every time I get on a plane, I imagine what it would be like to travel in First Class. I always make a point to pause, as if I'm about to travel to the front of the plane and I'm working on decluttering negative beliefs I about travelling First Class (it's a waste of money, it's not worth it, etc.). It's not something I've made an upgrade to straight away, I'm practicing with upgrading my seat selection and there are other things I'm working on first (my car for example).

It's incredibly fun to find something new and symbolic to upgrade!

This is why I preach this important message - you don't have to win the lottery to achieve your dreams. There is nothing you can do to make it happen, except to buy a ticket and hope.

You are much better off making small upgrades in your everyday life because you'll feel like you can control your success and take actions towards it. You can take a small action several times a day (I recommend taking action several times an hour - either by activating one of your automatic reminders or writing down your goals). Imagine if you bought a lottery ticket every hour or even every day? That would give you a gambling addiction.

It's not necessary to win the lottery because you can create even more magic in your life by your simple, every day actions, and the Universe always rewards action. What are you going to do TODAY to upgrade your life?

Practice Being Rich Now

I made one of my clients go and test-drive some cars to see was it would *feel* like to be able to drive the car of her dreams. She wasn't even really looking for a new car but she needed a breakthrough from her previous mindset of, *"We can't afford it so we won't bother even looking"*.

While this seems like it's not a big leap just to test drive a car, you have to do anything and everything to actually believe you deserve to be a VIP.

I'm not a big fan of spending all of your money on just one outrageously expensive item at the cost of everything else. When Mark and I lived in a cheap London neighbourhood, we'd see people with terrible cheap houses but the biggest flat-screen T.V. ever. I think it's obscene to spend money you don't have on luxury goods, especially if the rest of your life is crap. That's why I love the incremental upgrade. You start with whatever is bugging you first and take it to the very next level. That way you build your wealth mindset with a really solid foundation with few gaps on the way to being rich.

And until the money shows up, do whatever you can do to get you closer to being in your First Class life. Go and stand in the store with that super expensive leather lounge you've always wanted. Sit on the lounge for a few minutes every week and really *feel* what it would be like to have that beautiful piece of furniture in your home. As you sit there, put your hand on your heart and affirm to the Universe - *"I'm ready for a First Class life"*.

Go in to a nice department store and pretend you can buy anything in the store, you're just *choosing* not to today. Ask questions about different items, try things on and feel the difference. Learn to be discerning and figure out what your taste actually would be if money wasn't an issue. Decide exactly what colour and style you'd have, based on your own preference not the price tag.

"It's that first step – getting out the door – that's the toughest. If you can do that, you've already won."
Mary J. Blige

When I was an event planner at age 25, I'd always go and look at the most expensive hotels and conference rooms, even if it was out of my client's budget just to see what it felt like. I pretended my colleague Phil was my personal assistant and maybe they saw right through me, but it helped me feel more comfortable around luxury.

The Billionaire's Phone

There are some things that you'll upgrade to the point where you reach a limit. For example, you can have the same phone as a billionaire; an iPhone. Literally, if you had all the money in the world, you'd still probably *choose* to have an iPhone.

You might still shop for food the same way, choosing organic produce and expensive tomatoes. So you've reached the limit of your food upgrade and you don't have to keep finding ways to upgrade for the sake of it. First Class for you doesn't always have to mean the most expensive.

When you reach the pinnacle of what you'd probably choose if you were a billionaire, then pick something else to upgrade.

> *"Money won't buy happiness, unless we exchange it for the things that will bring happiness. If we don't know how to get any happiness out of five dollars, we won't know how to get it out of five hundred, or five thousand, or five hundred thousand."*
> Eleanor H. Porter

Sometimes you have to ease your way to feeling wealthy, but you'll start to see that buying quality is really the only way to go, and it saves so much energy making the decision once to have a First Class life. Go without before buying cheap.

Being Cheap with Yourself

We sometimes try to make things difficult for ourselves because we're reluctant to pay the money for the right solution, because maybe we think we should do it ourselves or deep down, we don't believe we deserve the very best.

An example of this in my own life was when something happened to our carpets resulting in two giant, gross-smelling stains (I refuse to say what or who caused the stains, but let's say it wasn't me). We tried to clean it ourselves, but it didn't totally come out so it was still visible and a little bit smelly. Every time I walked into the room, I could see it. It was lingering in the back of my mind as one of those little annoyances. It definitely didn't make me feel rich!

Finally after three days of staring at those stains, I called a cleaning company who specialise in deep cleaning carpets. They came around with their giant machine, and in less than 15 minutes they had got it all out. It only cost $65.

Sixty five bucks to solve the problem, in fact, remove the problem completely and thus save me from looking at it or worrying about it ever again. But I have to admit, I was reluctant to pay it, thinking that I should be able to do it myself.

While I was coaching with clients I told this story repeatedly because as women entrepreneurs, we're often looking for the make-do fix. We feel like we "should" know how to do it alone. We not only polish the turd, we roll it in glitter for good measure.

**Polish a turd or roll it in glitter;
it's still shit and you deserve more.**

Where in your life are you trying to polish that turd? Maybe you are trying to do everything yourself for your business, from websites to P.R. or paying bits and pieces of money for cobbled together solutions that don't quite work.

Maybe you are waiting to get the new laptop /iPad/iPhone because you can't justify the expense yet or you don't feel ready for the best equipment.

Maybe you're driving a car that is falling apart and continuing to pay money to get it fixed instead of buying a new car. Or are you being loyal to a hairdresser or beauty therapist even if you aren't happy with their service anymore? Maybe you resent your partner because they buy new shoes and clothes when they need them without feeling guilty about it. Men tend to do that!

The good news is – every time you choose the VIP or upgraded option, every time you choose to honour yourself, your time and (let's face it) your mental health, the Universe rewards you.

Sometimes that costs money, sometimes it's inconvenient and yes, sometimes you will feel guilty. But in the end you are being true to yourself and valuing yourself, and by doing this you will only attract more of these positive experiences.

The beautiful thing about this is you can take action on it straight away. Pick one thing today in your day to day life that is causing unnecessary wasted energy and immediately upgrade it. Call the cleaning company and book them in. Book in the virtual assistant. Lock in the date for the new headshots. Go through your closet and chuck out everything that's Economy and budget. Do it before you're ready.

This will have a huge impact on your manifesting ability – show the Universe that you are worth more and you'll be rewarded for it.

You might think that you'll save money by buying a cheap pair of shoes, but in the long run you will probably end up spending more because they just don't fit you right and they won't make you feel fabulous, so you'll always be looking for that next pair.

My client Claire chose to upgrade her clothes on the last round of the Money Bootcamp, and decided to buy the "expensive jeans" instead of her usual, even though a part of her didn't think she was the type of person to buy that brand.

"I just wear them over and over again, knowing they look amazing. It saves me even having to look in shops or worry about how they look, because I know they are perfect," Claire said.

Upgrade your wardrobe and see a stylist, another activity I always thought that only rich women could afford. It's actually not that expensive but it saves you time, money and effort because you know the clothes they choose for you will look good, fit you well and will suit you. It will save you so much money in the end and you will feel like a fancy rich celebrity. You know how much fun it is to say "oh this dress? *My stylist* picked it out for me". It's hilariously fun practicing feeling rich and you don't have to be an asshole about it. In fact, confide in your friend how little it actually cost you and expand *her* awareness of what's possible for her too.

Sometimes putting yourself in luxurious situations might feel uncomfortable. You might judge the people around you in the Jaguar showroom or you notice weird rich lady plastic surgery in the fancy tea room. Remember, you can be the exact type of rich person you like. Don't even pretend to shop in places you wouldn't anyway.

If you're experiencing resistance around something like this, it's not because the Universe is saying *"That's for everyone else and not for you"*, the resistance is coming out because there's still something there you haven't cleared.

Go back and declutter a belief or judgement you have around money or rich people.

Learn to feel good about spending money on things that bring you pleasure. Support local businesses, make ethical choices and encourage others to do the same. Be generous with yourself first and you'll become richer for it. Then you can create good in the world through your generosity too. Every upgrade action shows the Universe you are worthy of living an abundant life.

Chapter Summary

- You can't manifest when you feel poor
- Upgrade your life incrementally to feel richer every day
- What would the millionaire version of you choose?
- Practice being rich and generous now to try on your version of a First Class life

$

Dealing With Your Money Sabotages

"Each of us guards a gate of change that can only be unlocked from the inside."
Marilyn Ferguson

You have the best of intentions to change your life and you're proud of yourself for embracing this new Lucky Bitch lifestyle. You've been forgiving like a mofo, you've put a million positive reminders into your iPhone and you're religiously tracking every single cent. You even picked up money off the street. I'm proud of you!

And then one day…

You get an speeding fine or crash your car
You owe the tax man instead of the expected refund
Your relationship goes to shit
Your computer craps itself and dies
You suddenly go up two dress sizes

What the hell is going on?!

Denise – you told me to forgive all the assholes in my past, I threw away all of my clothes and bought some fancy schmancy hand-soap. I'm muttering my affirmations on the train like a crazy person and now my life is falling apart? I'm going to burn this stupid book. Thanks for nothing.

Hold yer horses pardner. It's just your sabotages talkin'.

Here's the good news, girlfriend. Get through this temporary wonky period and you'll make a huge leap forward. It's just a test. Just your old zits coming up because you're cleaning everything out.

Your sabotages are your default fear pattern when things are going too good. It's that pesky feeling like you've stretched your elastic too far and you PING back into your old reality.

I have my own sabotaging behaviours which I've worked hard to recognise and stop. When I was a kid, if something good happened, I was sure that something bad was about to happen. As an adult I continued with this self-fulfilling mindset. Whenever anything good happened like a new client, a promotion, a cute guy asked me out, I'd feel good for about five seconds and then I would feel sick, because I would be waiting for the "piano to fall on my head". That's why so many bad things happened, I totally manifested them!

When I was in my twenties there was much less drama in my life than my childhood, but my body was still kind of craving it in some way. My ego was still craving it, so I created self-sabotaging behaviours. One thing I would do was over-eat until I felt sick. I would also get bored in my job and let things slip so I would sabotage my career. I went out with guys who were all wrong for me and I stayed way too long in toxic friendships.

"There's an inherent thing in me where, if things are going too smooth, I'll sabotage the hell out of them, just to make the music more of a sanctuary."
Daniel Johns of *Silverchair*

Another one of my sabotaging behaviours is perfectionism. Living by the rule *"it has to be perfect or not at all"*, really cost me a lot over the years because I just wouldn't take action unless it was exactly right. For example some days it feels like a lot of hard work to put on make-up and do my hair when I have videos to make from home. Part of me says *"You can't appear in a video looking like crap, people will judge you"*.

Previously, I would never have made a video if I really didn't feel like getting "dressed up". Now I just try to circumnavigate those self-sabotaging behaviours and ask myself, "what's the worst that could happen?". And of course we know what would happen – nothing, who cares! So I push through that sabotaging behaviour by just getting on with it and making those videos straight out of bed in my pyjamas!

Your Default Sabotaging Behaviours

Many women suffer from what I call RSI – *Repetitive Sabotage Injury* because we're so predictable and we've all got our own personal blend of sabotage that we repeat until we've learned the lesson.

Maybe you create more bills for yourself like speeding

fines or parking fines because you don't pay attention. Maybe you leave it too late to do your taxes and so you get the inevitable fine. Maybe you know that your accountant isn't First Class, so you aren't getting all the deductions you really deserve. I encourage people to repeat the Money Bootcamp several times because you find new ways of identifying your sabotaging patterns. They show up in different and creative ways as you hit new income ceilings.

"I have a tendency to sabotage relationships and everything else in my life. Fear of success, fear of failure, fear of being afraid. Useless, good-for-nothing thoughts."
Michael Bublé

Why the hell do we do this?

Play around with your self-awareness to figure out why you're creating this drama in your life. Yes - you totally are, but it's not your fault.

I think the two quotes I used above are really interesting because I long suspected Daniel Johns and Michael Bublé of sabotaging their relationships. Daniel is divorced from fellow Australian Natalie Imbruglia, one of the most beautiful women in the world, and he suffered from anorexia and arthritis at the peak of his career that prevented him from touring. Weirdly enough, one of our trips on the Honeymoon Testers was to their secret wedding venue in Queensland.

Michael Bublé was engaged to the gorgeous Emily Blunt (he wrote his Grammy Award-nominated single *Everything* for her) but reportedly cheated on her. Classic sabotage.

This form of self-sabotage seems to happen a lot for celebrity marriages. Deep down the sabotage happens when he (or she) doesn't believe they really deserve happiness as well as fame and money. It's all too much, so they sabotage it to feel more comfortable with what they think they really deserve.

Let's speculate for a moment...

Maybe you keep your life Economy Class to avoid upsetting somebody in your life. You don't want the perceived negative consequences of having a lot of money because unconsciously you think something "bad" could happen to you. You don't want to piss people off. You don't want to draw attention to yourself. You don't want to have extra responsibility. You don't want to create more dramas in your life or jealousy from other people. It would be a drag to pay more taxes. Your brother/mother/best friend will get upset. People will think you're a bitch.

Any of these hitting home?

Fear of Saying No

Saying no to requests around money is totally ok. You don't need to be responsible for others, it's fine to deny their request and let them figure out for themselves how they are going to afford what it is they want. While doing my Money Bootcamp course, one of my clients, Alana, realised she had taken on the role of financial rescuer because she couldn't say no to lending money to others.

"I had always identified with not having enough money but when I did the hidden treasures exercise during the Money

Bootcamp, I added up $25,000 that I have lent to people and have never asked for it back. I realised this came from my dad as I've seen him as the strong dependable breadwinner and it doesn't matter how much he's got, he's always willing to lend a hand," Alana said.

On one hand it's a lovely quality to be so generous, but on the other hand it's a lot of money to not have in your own bank account. It was such an ingrained response for her to say yes to these requests we did some digging to see where that came from.

"I get the feeling that I'm doing the right thing by helping out others and that I'm being the good girl and being responsible. I guess it comes from when I was growing up and my mother was sick (and I had to look after her). I have over extended my responsibility my entire life," Alana said.

We looked at ways that Alana could take back her power and begin to feel more comfortable with saying no to lending money. I asked Alana to role play situations with me where people would ask her for money. Even though it was just "pretend", she had trouble saying no to me. She felt terrible and guilty, but it became easier over time and then she could practice saying no in her real life.

It might feel strange to practice these types of conversations but the more you practice it, the more comfortable you will be when you need to actually say no in real life, so have a friend play along with you.

"Friendship and money: oil and water."
Mario Puzo

When these requests for money pop up, and you do have the money available but you don't actually want to lend it out, it's ok to say no.

What are you afraid of? That they'll hate you, call you a bitch or create even more drama in their life? What about if you call and ask for it back, what are you afraid of?

As usual, this gives you incredible information to add to your forgiveness list.

I Can't Break Through My Income Level!

When you hit a new level of income resistance, don't hide away, it's time to go one step deeper, even deeper than before. You have most likely uncovered so many past experiences and your body is probably going through some serious changes and energetic shifts. As you're raising your energetic vibration around money sometimes the physical body has to catch up. It can make you feel a little bit weird. If you're feeling out of sorts, out of body, or feel like you're just on another planet, it's completely normal. Just be gentle with yourself and identify your sabotaging patterns without blaming yourself.

When You Get "Too" Lucky

When you're manifesting like a mofo and you're winning, winning, winning all the time, it will get to a point when you think, "Is this too much? Can anyone really be this lucky?"

It's exactly like in ***Peter Pan,*** when everyone is learning to fly by thinking happy thoughts. As soon as you let the doubt creep in, you start to fall.

I went through two years of winning everything I entered; scholarships, free courses, and of course, the six months all-expenses-paid travel and I did start to get some negative feedback. It was kind of freaking me out a little bit and it got to the point that I just didn't want to tell anyone about my winnings anymore or the fact that I was super lucky. I started to get embarrassed and I stopped thinking happy thoughts.

This was not good for my manifesting mojo and sure enough, I stopped winning so much. I needed to be really one-minded with my positivity so that anyone who tried to side-track me, consciously or unconsciously, wouldn't be able to throw me off course on my way to reaching my goals.

I was at an event run by my mentor Sandy Forster and I started chatting with the woman seated beside me. I told her how I win everything and that I was going to win one of the lucky door prizes. She was totally impressed and inspired, but as soon as I told her, I started to feel sick about it.

I sat there thinking, *"what if I win? This woman is going to think I'm selfish for winning everything. Maybe I've won so much that I should just give other people a chance"*.

Then I thought, *"what if I* don't *win? I told her that I'm lucky and I win all the time, she's going to think I'm a fraud"*. All those little seeds of self-doubt started to creep into my mind.

Let me tell you, it's virtually impossible to consciously manifest success when you're freaking out. So, when the time came for the draw of the first prize, I knew that if I really did want to win, I had to push the negativity out of my mind and replace it with positive thoughts. I didn't want the Universe tuning into those negative fears, so I wrote down on my piece of paper, *"It's okay for me to win, it's okay for good things to happen to me all the time"*.

I sat with it and I felt peace in my heart about the outcome. Either way, I would be safe. I did a little bit of EFT tapping on my hand under my table, saying to myself "even though I win all the time, I deeply and completely love and accept myself".

As I was tapping away discreetly under my table, the winner was announced. It was me! The woman next to me said, "oh my God, you do win everything!"

When you're having these sorts of negative thoughts, you just *can't* tune into them. Don't pay them any attention.

If you start to get dragged down by other people's reactions to your good fortune just remember that your wealth is your responsibility alone. You can't get side-tracked from your journey by worrying about what other people think.

"The only way not to think about money is to have a great deal of it."
Edith Wharton

You do deserve to win all the time. You do deserve to be lucky and you do deserve to be successful and live the life you dream about.

Giving Up Money Responsibility

When I was 20 or so, I lived in a grungy student flat in Sydney. I was from a small town so moving to Sydney was a big deal for me. I had upgraded from an even grungier flat where I lived in the shed outside for $50 a week, so this new place was virtually a palace in comparison.

I lived with a few friends, one let's call *Stacy.* I loved Stacy. She was the perfect slacker housemate. She rarely went to Uni so some days we'd hang out playing card games and eating cheese on toast while watching *Friends* or *Bring it On.* Stacy was responsible for paying the rent, which in those days we did in cash. At the start of the month we'd each give her $400 in cash and she went to the bank to deposit it... old school. Only turns out – she didn't always go straight to the bank. Sometimes she spent it and replaced it days later or not at all. But none of us knew that she was stealing our money.

About six months after Stacey took on this important responsibility, we got a call from the landlord telling us completely out of the blue that we were being evicted unless we coughed up thousands of dollars in unpaid rent. When we confronted Stacey, she admitted to it immediately but I felt so betrayed. She was supposed to be my friend and she stole from me. It sucked.

It was a harsh lesson, but you know what... I didn't really learn anything from it; in fact, I barely expressed my disappointment to her at all. She paid the money and moved out, but this wasn't the only time I gave my money power away or ignored money problems. I could give you numerous examples like getting into massive amounts of credit card debt or spending all my money windfalls really quickly instead of saving it. I didn't even open my credit card statements for years.

There are many ways that women give away their power around money. Sometimes it takes a crisis to actually wake you up to it, other times it's incredibly subtle.

One of my Bootcamp ladies, Jess, always seemed to

pay for her friends when they went out for coffee or even lunch. It got to the point when her friends wouldn't even offer to pay anymore and just waited until Jess reached for the cheque. She was getting resentful about it, but couldn't say anything because she felt like a bitch. Annoying right?

During my Money Bootcamp, Jess realised that this was an *old* pattern, going back to childhood where she gave away her pocket money to others. She felt bad and almost guilty that she earned more money than her friends and felt like it was her responsibility to pay for them.

I set her an assignment. Next time the restaurant bill came, she had to sit and wait (on her hands if she had to). She couldn't be the first to make the move. She couldn't automatically offer even if it was excruciatingly awkward. It was tough for her at first, but then she realised other things about her friends. They sat and bitched about money the whole lunch and she went away from their meetups, not only resentful about their cheap-ass ways but feeling deflated and depressed about money. Bad feelings attract more bad feelings.

You know what? Her friends didn't change their behaviour but Jess did - she had to transition her friendships to people who had the kind of money relationship she wanted.

Where do you take more responsibility with money than you need to?

On the other extreme, Beth realised that she wasn't taking any responsibility around money at all. Her husband paid for everything. She just put her income into a single joint account and let him organise all the bills. She never opened a single one, until she found out later they were in thousands of unexpected credit card debt.

Funnily enough, it was an old family pattern. Her dad had left her mother with massive amounts of totally unexpected debt when he died.

Where are you giving up money responsibility in your life?

Taking power back around your money is about getting the balance right. Taking too much or too little responsibility holds you back from having a beautiful, healthy and abundant relationship with your true wealthy self.

You don't need to get evicted, lose all your friends or break up your marriage to learn the lesson. Take a look at where money is a pain in the butt for you and ask yourself:

- *Where has this shown up in the past?*
- *What's the pattern? What's the Universe trying to tell you?*
- *What are you afraid of?*
- *What are you no longer willing to put up with?*

These simple, but magic questions will uncover your personal blend of sabotage and once you figure out the lesson, you can clear it *forever.*

Look for Recurring Patterns

We really are creatures of habit and our saboteurs really aren't that creative. If you're not sure exactly how you're holding yourself back, look for recurring patterns in your life around money.

They aren't always easy to see because you're so *used* to them. It's just "how life is" or you feel like you have no control over it. Maybe it's "their fault".

It's like the friend who attracts the same bad boyfriend every time and wonders why it ended the exact same way as last time. What's the common denominator in the way money dramas come up in your life? YOU!

One of my clients had a really annoying situation happen with a tradesman during the Money Bootcamp, which on the surface seemed like a one-off kind of thing. But after we peeled back a few layers, Melissa realised that she had repeatedly been bullied and ripped off by various people throughout her life and these repetitive episodes were holding her back from being truly wealthy. She almost always paid more than she should, felt resentful about it and the work was often shoddy and cost her much more in the long run anyway. Of course, she justified it in perfectly rational sounding ways:

All tradesmen are dodgy anyway.
These guys never know what they're doing.
People will always try and rip you off.
I should speak up, it's my fault.
It's hard to find a good tradesman.
I'm so unlucky with repairs!

By doing some forgiveness work on *herself* as well as the various dodgy guys she'd hired in the past, Melissa was willing to look at why she had been creating these situations with repairman as a recurring sabotage.

We dug deeper into the last time it happened, when her dishwasher broke. The minute the repairman walked through the door she felt that his energy was just so wrong, but she couldn't put her finger on it. He was condescending with her and she felt uncomfortable even having him in the house. But she felt like she couldn't complain and when he started to give a detailed explanation about an expensive part for the dishwasher, she felt her confidence shrink and even though it sounded dodgy as hell, she agreed.

Then he made a massive deal about being paid upfront for the parts and then didn't answer her calls for days. All week she was mentally kicking herself for giving in to the bully.

When I asked her how it felt, Melissa said that she felt massive anger towards him, but almost blocked and powerless to do anything about it. I asked her to dig deep and see if it reminded her of anything else in her life, even if it didn't seem immediately connected.

Melissa told me that when she moved out of home and was starting to earn money in her career, her brother got into trouble with drugs and it got to the point where he would come to her house late at night begging and then demanding money to pay off his various gambling and drug debts. It would quickly turn abusive when she refused, calling her a "selfish bitch" and worse because he knew she had the money. Sometimes she'd feel so bad that she'd give him a few hundred dollars. Immediately, her brother would be all smiles and full of promises to pay it back. A few times she refused and he kicked her garage door in or threatened to kill her dog.

Because he was her brother, she never called the cops but felt sick about it every time. It was that same sense of powerlessness that still lived in her body and was being triggered by these repairmen, disrespecting and bullying her about money.

It was a very similar situation, she felt bullied, and obligated to pay him without getting anything in return. Then we looked even further back and Melissa realised her alcoholic dad did the same thing.

"I was 16 and I had a part time job at the local shop. If my dad was short of cash, he would ask me to take my money out of my piggie bank and would never repay it," Melissa said.

She had this enormous sense of *"this isn't* fair!" but because she loved her dad, she never said anything to him.

Even though Melissa is a capable adult woman now, those memories still live within her and made her totally unconsciously decide something about the world:

Life's not fair!
Men rip me off.
Nobody will take care of me.
Everything will be taken from me.
I have to give in or I'll get in trouble.

You might think I'm being overly dramatic but I've seen the powerful financial transformation that women create when they eliminate *anything* from their past that affects their current self-esteem.

Where something keeps showing up in your awareness, it's happening for a reason. It's bringing your attention to something you should clear, either a memory from the past or a traumatic event that created a new limiting self-belief.

Melissa wouldn't have felt safe being any wealthier because it would have created even more situations where people who were supposed to love and take care of her, actually took advantage and abused her. Being able to clear that old memory created a little more space for more abundance in her life in a way that could make her feel powerful instead of bullied.

It's amazing when you figure out the lesson, because it's an A-HA moment that illuminates your weird behaviour or your "unluckiness" in a particular situation. Learn it and say to the Universe, *"I get it. You can stop beating me over the head with it now"*.

Forgive the people involved, including yourself. Forgive yourself for allowing it to happen or enabling it. Forgive yourself for being a "coward" and letting others take away your power. Forgive your parents or ex-husband for taking your money. Forgive, forgive, forgive.

Give yourself permission to be rich without being ripped off, without having to be bullied into giving it to others and allowing yourself to feel safe.

By doing some healing work you will be able to break the cycle of repeatedly creating the situation. Learn the lesson and move on, just feel it lift off your shoulders and leave it behind forever.

How Much Wealth Are You Really Entitled to?

Many of my Bootcamp participants have great success in the beginning and then they'll inevitably hit a wall and feel like "it's too much". That's when the sabotaging, back-tracking and doubt start to screw with your manifesting plans. You sabotage yourself by attracting unexpected bills, speeding fines, unwanted debts and money feels tighter than ever. You doubt that this manifesting stuff even works. You quit and give up.

That's why you're fighting with your partner over something really dumb or spending money you don't have on things you don't need. It's not about the money at all.

Boom – you've just crashed into your energetic income level.

You've reached a limit to what you believe is possible.

The same thing happens if you're going really well on your diet, you start to get more attention, you start to feel good about yourself… then it feels strangely weird. So you go to the fridge and eat a whole cake without knowing *why*. Anything to numb that fear.

> *"It's not about the money, money, money We don't need your money, money, money We just wanna make the world dance Forget about the price tag."*
> Jessie J, *Price Tag*

As Gay Hendricks talks about in his amazing book *The Big Leap,* you've uncovered your own personal Upper Limit Problem, a "negative emotional reaction that occurs when anything positive enters our lives and leads to self-destructive behaviours. The Upper Limit Problem not only prevents happiness, but it actually stops us from achieving our goals".

This awesome book taught me more about my money sabotages than any book about wealth. So, when something "bad" happens, don't convince yourself that you're not meant to lead a life of outrageous success and unbelievable wealth – you're just experiencing an upper limit problem.

We're not all motivated by money and we are not all motivated by material things. You don't have to be a millionaire to live an amazing life. Your energetic income level might be $50,000 right now, it could be a million. Work on everything in this book and it will be something different six months down the track. The point is, it doesn't hurt to dream plus it's okay to be as rich as you want. That panic, that guilt that comes up, even hypothetically? That's valuable information to clear and declutter, so you can create more abundance in the real world.

Hannah was in a tight spot financially and she and her husband had said to each other "don't do anything big", in terms of gifts, but then her husband gave her a really amazing present at Christmas. She had this immediate gut reaction of "I really don't deserve this". Instead of feeling good, the experience made her feel *horrible.*

When Hannah thought about it further she realised she didn't feel good about the present because her past still lived with her. Her dad had abandoned her family and this experience made her believe at a really early age that she didn't deserve her father's love, money, protection and care. So this seemingly innocent experience bumped up against what she thought was possible and what she was "allowed" to have. Guess what she did – forgave and released.

"It is not the man who has too little, but the man who craves more, that is poor."
Seneca

Memories of divorce and nasty fights over child support come up a lot for my clients. They saw their parents bicker about the amount of child support the other parent "deserved" and many women now use that memory as energetic "proof" that they're not worth it.

"When I look at women who I think have it all, I label them as a 'bitch', and then I feel this mild repulsion towards them because they appear self-entitled and spoilt. Everything my dad thought of my mum for wanting child support," says my client Cassie.

Even though warring parents bring their own baggage to the conversation, the child feels like that's what they are "worth", even though one parent might have been actually trying to punish the other by using money as the weapon. The child though, wonders if there is something wrong with them that their dad (mainly) doesn't want to pay money to support them.

All children should feel entitled to unconditional love and safety. When our parents hurt us at a very young age, it messes up our future energetic income *and* happiness level. When things feel "too good", it triggers all those old feelings of confusion and unworthiness.

If this is triggering memories of your own parent's divorce, add all of these new realisations to your forgiveness list and just get rid of them.

You Control the Meaning of Your Story

When I did Landmark Education, a powerful course in integrity, I learnt a powerful truth. Humans like to make meaning out of everything. As Landmark says, "we are meaning making machines".

Your story shapes your energetic income level, it's the origin of most of your personal sabotages and at worst, it plays out repeatedly until you learn the lesson.

You know that strong emotion attracts your goals to you quickly, but only YOU have the power to choose whether you attract positivity or negativity. The Universe doesn't care, it will bring you what it thinks you are asking for. If you're constantly living with the program of "I'm so broke", it will create situations for you where you can justify being broke, hence the unexpected bills and money upsets.

You can choose to stop your sabotaging behaviour in its tracks and transform fear into power. You can even say out loud *"Hello old friend. I see you and I know what you're doing. Now fuck off"*.

My client, Becca, had a customer who wanted a refund for a thousand dollar course and it freaked her out. Immediately she was worried that if she did give this guy a refund, all of a sudden, five other people were going to ask for their money back too. She started to doubt her ability as a coach. She started to worry herself sick that her course was too expensive and then it spiralled into her old self-defeating pattern.

I'm not worth it.
I don't deserve to be successful.
There's something wrong with me.
<u>Everyone</u>'s going to ask for their money back.

If Becca had let her old sabotage escalate, it might have happened. Together we stopped that train of thought dead in its tracks. I asked her *"what kind of gift is this guy giving you?"*, because trust me, situations like this are always a gift in disguise and an opportunity to break through the next level of income. Whatever happens, whether it's a tax bill, your car needs fixing, it's exactly the lesson you need to identify and eliminate your sabotage.

By halting the default sabotaging behaviour, you can start to look at practical considerations. When we removed the "*I'm not good enough*" story her ego was trying to pull, we had practical and non-judgemental stuff to work on. Becca needed to tighten up her refund policy and put steps into place to ensure she attracted the right customers into her business in the first place. She could hire a customer service person to deal with refund enquiries and she could create a refund procedure instead of freaking out every time. She could track her refund rates to ensure they were in line with industry averages and only then look at why people were refunding. Becca made herself move out of fear mode and look objectively at the situation and why she reacted the way she did. When you do that once, your sabotages lose their grip over you.

If Becca had stayed in panic mode there would have been a lot of emotional charge attached to the situation and she could've made it really messy, not only by creating more refunds but by creating money drama in all areas of her life like manifesting an unexpected tax bill, crashing her car or picking a fight with her husband. By dropping the fear and choosing to look at it as a gift meant she learned the lesson the Universe was trying to give her and she moved on.

"Money is not the most important thing in the world.
Love is. Fortunately, I love money."
Jackie Mason

The Sacrifices You Have to Make to Be Rich

In my twenties, while I ran around experimenting with my career and businesses, a friend said to me, *"You'd do anything for money, wouldn't you?"* This came after I told her the hilarious (I thought) story about taking part in a medical experiment testing drugs for money.

My first thought was *"I didn't have a choice, I had to pay my University tuition. What a bitch!"* I thought it was funny to tell the story about the medical experiment – how I was testing a morphine based drug and willed myself not to throw up in case I got kicked out of the experiment.

My friend was appalled that I would risk my health for a few thousand bucks, but I was secretly proud of myself for "doing whatever it took" to earn money to take care of myself, not realising it was my pattern and my own brand of sabotage. My underlying story was:

I'm all alone.
I have to take care of myself.
Nobody loves me.
I'm willing to do what it takes.

I literally couldn't see another way to earn the money than to do something other people weren't willing to do. I was proud of it!

When I extended that thinking to becoming rich, I had similar beliefs:

You have to do unethical things to be rich.
You have to work really hard.
It's wrong to love money.
It's going to be a painful road.
I have to do it all by myself.

I have to be willing to do what it takes.

You might intellectually think you want to be rich but your underlying story will create a self-fulfilling prophecy for you. It *will* be hard, lonely and painful if you believe it will be.

You might believe that you have to sacrifice time with your family to be really successful, or skip going to the gym to put in more hours at the office to get your income to that next level. You might believe that you'll lose all your friends, that your family will ask you for money, that you'll have to pay more taxes, that your children will get kidnapped for ransom and lots of other bad things.

Yep – they all sound slightly ridiculous when you *intellectually* think about them, but if you have even a teeny tiny fear around money, the Universe never wants to put you in danger, so you will actively and unconsciously repel money from your life.

Are you willing to let it be easy?

One of my clients, Candice, felt as if she couldn't have it all, like good skin, money, *and* a great career. She felt it was too much.

She also felt like she had to work hard <u>now</u> so she could have a good time later in life.

"I used to get $50 a week pocket money. When you're a young person that's quite a lot of money. The one thing my Dad used to always say to me was "make sure you save it for later in life, don't spend it all now." I would sneak away and spend it. Even growing up through my teens I would always spend it because I was told not to.

They also used to say *"make sure you stay in your full time job, work till you're 65"."*

This theme of "you can't have it now, you can't have it all, don't enjoy it now" was recurring throughout her life. Once she cleared that memory with EFT and forgiveness, she added an affirmation;

"I deserve to enjoy life now, *I'm worth spending money on* now.*"*

It doesn't matter if you grew up rich or poor, seemingly inconsequential memories like this can totally affect how you deal with money as an adult and what you believe you have to sacrifice to be rich and happy.

"Money should not cost you your joy."
Laurence G. Boldt

Even though we all have a past and we all have some baggage, your financial future is entirely on your own terms. Every part of your success and your journey is negotiable - every single part of it.

It's Safe to Be Powerful

Some of the women I see who are on the verge of success have been told throughout their life that their natural leadership ability or personal power is "wrong". This really pisses me off because considering some of the unethical and horrible rich people in the world, the women I know who are gorgeous, smart and creative are the ones who *should* be rich because they would change the world for the better. They just needed to declutter their feelings around being powerful and allow themselves to feel safe to show up bigger in the world.

I hit a big issue in my second year of business when I found it really hard to employ people. I knew that to go past six figures, I couldn't do everything myself, but it *terrified* me.

So, I experimented and hired a few people on a trial basis. It would go okay for a while then the person would unexpectedly rip me off, not do the work properly or otherwise not work out. I once hired someone but didn't give her any direction or tasks. I actually told her that she could work whatever hours she wanted. She never did the work but I kept paying her… for twelve weeks. Talk about a boundaries problem!

I knew this was probably a recurring sabotage in my life, so I took some time to see what had happened in the past that was blocking me from receiving help, accepting help, and being the leader I wanted to be. BINGO! It didn't take me long to figure it out.

There have been lots of times in my life where I was the leader, but I got really negative feedback from taking charge. I used to start clubs when I was about eight or nine with all my friends. I just was a natural leader, so I always wanted to be the president of the cool kids club. I remember that sometimes the other kids would say, *"You're so bossy, Denise!"*. That was probably before we knew the word "bitch" but that's kind of what they meant.

The same thing happened at school. I would always take on leadership roles, like organising our end of year dance (prom), being on the fundraising committee, the year book committee and I was the dance captain of our performance group.

I was really organised and great at seeing what needed

to be done, but I'd feel terrible if any of the other girls said anything slightly negative like, *"Why does it have to be like that?"* or *"Who put you in charge?"*. So, I made it mean that being the leader was a bad thing.

At University I joined AIESEC, an international student organisation with lots of opportunities for leadership at a local, national or international level. By this time I had become extremely reluctant to take on any leadership roles in case I was criticized in anyway. However, people would single me out and say, *"Denise, you really should run for this position"*, but I was just so reluctant to be the leader based on my experiences at high school. I thought that leadership was painful, that people would call me bossy or bitchy if I took charge. I thought it was easier to tag along with everyone else, but my natural leadership ability made people turn to me for answers.

Then, the president of my local AIESEC chapter stepped down suddenly and I was kind of forced into the role. Maybe the Universe intervened to make me step up, but I was extremely uncomfortable with telling people what to do. By that stage, I probably had better management skills, so I wasn't being bossy and bitchy, but the same emotions were surfacing, that fear of "people will think I'm a bitch". I had to fire one of my executive team members and he actually *did* call me a bitch. It was horrible.

So, whenever I've had to step up, be the leader and make decisions, I've always had these types of feelings. I've realised all these past experiences meant I made huge mistakes with virtually no boundaries in place. When I hired that one woman, I basically left it up to her to decide what work she would take on or not. I pretty much said to her *"do whatever you want"*, because I didn't want to take control and be seen as a bitch. I was scared of telling her what to do in case she didn't like it. So I paid her every week and she did no work for me. Why would she? I had no energetic boundaries in place and attracted her to teach me the lesson.

Just when I should have been stepping up and taking charge of my own business, I was completely sabotaging it because I was running my old pattern. I was suffering from RSI – repetitive sabotage injury.

Now I could've kept blaming it on the people I was hiring or chalked it up to "unlucky" hires but I wouldn't have learnt the lesson and it would have kept showing up in other ways, costing me valuable time and lots of money in my business. I knew there were clues to my sabotaging behaviour in my past and it took me about 5 seconds to trace it back to those days as a bossy little girl.

By the way, notice how my greatest fear was being called a bitch and what did I end up calling my entire company?! Interesting, right?

So, to remove my "leadership sabotage", I did my forgiveness work and EFT. I looked at all those negative memories around being called a bitch, and bossy and forgave it all. I forgave myself for never wanting to step up and be the boss. I forgave other people for taking my money and not giving anything in return. I just sat with those memories and took myself back to those times and really felt the embarrassment and anger around them. Then I used that amazing little phrase: "I forgive you, I'm sorry and I love you".

That sabotage is long gone now!

Fear Of Being Centre Of Attention

Similar to the fear of being called a bitch, I had a client who didn't want to put herself forward for Class President in case the other kids thought she wanted to be the centre of attention. So as an adult she didn't do anything that would be considered being a show off.

We're told that the world doesn't revolve around us, that we're a "show-off" if we want attention or we're told to go sit in the corner and be quiet.

If this sounds like you, take a look at where that is showing up in your current life. What do you think about people who are the centre of attention? Do you think they are show-offs?

Where are you holding yourself back from being the centre of attention in your life or business? Would being rich put you in a highly visible situation where you might feel unsafe?

Where are you avoiding being seen, being admired, being respected, being followed, because of those early experiences of not wanting to be seen as being the centre of attention?

Maybe you're dying to be on T.V. but you don't want to be a show off, so you're avoiding valuable P.R. opportunities for your business.

Maybe the thought of walking down the aisle with everyone's eyes focused on you has been enough for you to unconsciously sabotage your relationships so you never get to the point of getting married?

Or, you wouldn't want to upgrade your house or car too much because other people in your family or neighbourhood will think badly of you.

I totally understand this way of thinking. I've avoided doing speaking gigs, especially in my local town, because it does make me feel uncomfortable being the centre of attention. I don't want people to think that I'm bossy, vain, or a show-off. I find it hard to take compliments for the same reason.

Money Follows the Path of Least Resistance

The easiest way to get rich is to do things that are natural to you. If you're a natural leader or dying to "perform" on T.V. you're doing yourself a huge disservice by denying your natural talent. The Universe is probably sending you these opportunities for a reason and you're pushing them back. You're pushing back the wealth.

Years ago, I looked at women in business winning awards and thought, "Wow! That's so cool, they must be really awesome at what they do". You know what? There's no secret to winning awards. Sometimes, there's not that much competition for them. For some you literally just have to put in an application and pay a fee. How easy is that? It's one of those things you just have to put yourself forward for and put in a nomination. Blow your own trumpet and be okay with being the centre of attention.

I recently had a photo shoot with a Cleo magazine, so I made myself take photos of it, and actually tell people about it even though I felt like I was showing off. I wasn't picked to be in Cleo because I was special. I just put in a pitch like anyone else and got selected. Some people don't ever apply because they psyche themselves out before they even get a chance.

Here's the thing. People will think you're stuck up no

matter what you do, so don't sabotage your success by hiding out. There is always going to be someone who thinks you suck. There are people who get a big ego boost from putting other people down. Just remember you're the kind of person who will see your success as it is. You'll enjoy it and appreciate it, but you won't make being the centre of attention a part of your identity. It's not going to turn you into a horrible vain monster. Trust that the Universe will only send you what you can handle and you'll still be a good person, no matter how successful and wealthy you'll get.

"Money is only a human invention. I get paid for my work, it's a system of trade, but it's not my purpose and reason for living."
Vanna Bonta

Chapter Summary

- Everyone has their own default money sabotages, it doesn't mean you can't be rich
- Self-awareness is the key to overcoming your sabotage. Tell the Universe that you've learnt the lesson and move on. Hand in your shovel and stop digging!
- Keep clearing and releasing as you discover new fears and recurring sabotages

Bonus - take the Money Sabotage test at www.GetRich LuckyBitch.com to see exactly where you are holding yourself back from being rich.

$

Who Is Really Holding You Back From Being Rich?

"The desire for riches is simply the capacity for a larger life seeking fulfilment."
Wallace Wattles

You probably have known at least one saboteur in your lifetime. You know, those people who try and subtly sabotage your diet by making you feel guilty for not ordering dessert or they make you feel bad for your success. They say underhanded things or backhanded compliments like:

Must be nice living high on the hog!
Alright for some!
You're so lucky, it's all been handed to you.
I could never sacrifice so much like you do.
My husband would never let me do that.
Must be hard to maintain all this success.

Basically your success is threatening them and so they behave like total dicks. Even people you thought would be thrilled for your success. It sucks because this fear will activate that part of your brain that thinks

"I will be shunned from the village,"
"I will be burnt as a witch,"
"I will be rejected and die".

So you hold yourself back, sabotage your own success and generally do anything you can to go along with other people. That's why it's so important to surround yourself with success; we are so influenced by the people around us.

I've had friends bitch about me behind my back, belittle my success to my face, tell me never to talk about my business again, uninvite me to their wedding, tell me I'm greedy, criticise my house or my car, and basically be total bitches. It happens, so don't worry about it. It's virtually a rite of passage.

"If you lend someone $20, and never see that person again; it was probably worth it."
Anonymous

Maybe someone in your own family is directly and deliberately sabotaging your manifesting efforts, or maybe you've grown up around people who had a terrible attitude about money so they try and pull you down.

One of the questions I'm frequently asked is "How do you deal with other people's crap when you're trying to manifest more money?"

Things like:

- *My husband is being sooo negative about money, what do I do?*
- *My best friend doesn't want to talk to me anymore since my business started doing well*

- *My mother-in-law disapproves of my business*
- *My friend thinks I'm stuck up*
- *I can't stand my Dad moaning about money*
- *My sister owes me a lot of money, should I ask for it back?*

Let's get real for a second. You can't change anyone else and if this is happening, it's an energetic match for you in some way. Think of it as a mirror that's showing up your own fear and insecurity. You can't *selectively* believe that you are capable of creating your reality. You either believe it whole heartedly or you don't. Good or bad, you're creating it in some way.

It's a hard concept to accept, because why would you purposefully manifest bad crap in your life, what are you a masochist? Unfortunately, you've got to take responsibility for how it makes you feel because *they* are probably not going to change a bit.

Think about why that person is getting in your face, what do you think it's trying to teach you or show you? If you can work out the deeper emotional charge, you can start to unravel the lessons around it. Do some forgiveness work and let it go. It really is that simple.

Take responsibility, even for them!

Think about that person who is holding you back energetically. Who is that person? What do you blame them for? Maybe it's that they never support you, or they are weighing you down with their negativity. Turn it around. Take responsibility for those things for which you are blaming them.

So instead of "They are holding me back", replace it with "I am holding myself back". Can you see the difference? One is saying, "Oh, it's not fair", and the other one is saying, "Wow, it's only me who's holding me back from going to that next level". One feels like you are placing the blame on someone else and the other one feels empowering because you are taking responsibility.

Instead of "They never support me", think "I never support myself. I'm never fully in my own corner. I'm never 100% on-board with the things that I do".

When you start to say things like that, it's like your body starts to spark with the truth of it. When you face up to these things and take responsibility, it empowers you to take action. By blaming others, you are giving that power away to the other person. Taking responsibility back on your own terms will go a long way in showing the Universe you are ready for bigger and better things. Taking responsibility is like doing the forgiveness work. It unburdens you. When you are busy placing blame on those around you for your misfortunes, you are actively being focused on the negative. When you decide to take responsibility for what and who you think is holding you back, you start to release the negativity around it.

Gratitude Your Way to Wealth

Another way to transform your way of thinking is to feel gratitude for all those people who you believe are holding you back.

You might feel that your boss is holding you back from reaching your higher income level by not granting you a raise. Instead of becoming angry and resentful, try to feel gratitude for what's she's teaching you. It could be a valuable lesson in sticking up for your self-worth or a kick up the butt to actually quit your job. That's something to be grateful for!

Journal: Who will feel most threatened by my new income level?

Think of a particular person who might feel the most threatened, upset, and energetically unbalanced by you breaking through to that next income level. It doesn't matter what that next income level is and it doesn't matter if it's true or not. Just think of the person who you'd be most afraid to tell about your success. Who would think you were a snob?

It could be that you want to go from $50,000 to $100,000 or you're so close to $1 million you can almost smell it. There's always going to be someone who you perceive would be energetically threatened by your success.

Remember, this has *nothing* to do with them and everything to do with your *own* fear about what they would think.

Lindsay says "When I really thought about this, the person that came up for me shocked the hell out of me!

"It was when my husband got a promotion and my business was doing really well. I had two record months in a row and suddenly it hit me. My husband and I are now the richest people in our entire family on both sides. I thought it was kind of cool. Then when I dwelt on it a little more, for me, out earning even the richest person in my family brought up some strange feelings.

"In my family, my Dad's brother was always the biggest earner and was super generous. He'd always pay bills when we went out for dinner. He always had an amazing car and an amazing house.

"When I realised I had exceeded his income, I broke down sobbing. I was inconsolable about the fact that I was emasculating my uncle, because I was taking away his role as the richest person in our family. I loved him and the fear hit me like a ton of bricks.

"I realised that in reality, he'd be proud of me no matter what. Who am I to say it's going to emasculate somebody because I'm earning amazing money? Having cleared this with some EFT and through realising it and talking about it, I'm now comfortable with my income level and how that fits with my family. Once you realise it, it can all just lift off your shoulders."

Just pick one person that brings up discomfort for you. It could be your best friend. This could be someone who you've grown up with for a long time. You've always had similar incomes. You've had similar houses and similar cars, but suddenly you're starting to go beyond that income and she's staying where she is. You once had conversations based on, *"I wish we could quit our jobs or earn lots of money doing what we love"*, and then suddenly you're getting there and she's not. You might not want to make her feel bad or as if she is not working hard enough. So not only are you afraid to tell her about your success, you're now energetically holding yourself back from becoming even more rich.

Anastasia says, "My best friend is really creative and entrepreneurial but she just doesn't follow through on anything.

"In our twenties, we'd sit and talk about all our business ideas but did nothing about them. Suddenly, I got focused and started earning enough money to quit my job. I think she got sick of our conversations where instead of bitching about our jobs, I only had good news to report.

"She started accusing me of having no time for her, that I'd changed and she didn't like the new me. It really hurt because out of everyone in my life, I thought she'd be the happiest for me.

"In the end, I had to realise that I needed to be around successful people and just limit my exposure to people who would be jealous or negative due to their own stuff."

Unfortunately, this is a really common scenario. I don't advocate breaking up with friends, just don't let them be your excuse.

Another example of a saboteur could be someone in your family. Maybe you're worried that they think you'll become a snob. Maybe you're worried that they're going to mooch off you. That was a big one for me. I was thinking, *"God, if I'm the richest person in the family, I'm going to have to pay for dinner all the time"*. It wasn't true, it was just another bullshit excuse my ego told me to prevent me from making more money.

Who is it in your family who could be threatened by you really embracing your wealth?

What about your partner?

The next example is a juicy, juicy, juicy one. Your saboteur could be your husband, boyfriend, girlfriend or ex-partner. You could be worried that an ex-partner will come after your money or that you will become so wealthy that they will stop paying child support. That's another energetic fear that will hold you back from making more money.

You might worry that you'll emasculate your partner because you have a story that the man should be the breadwinner.

You might worry that being richer would cause you to break up. When you start to work on yourself and begin to grow really quickly, quite often the partner is just not willing to go where you want to go. This can totally suck and is a major reason women keep themselves small financially.

If your partner is holding you back, you need to have a conversation with them and share your goals and dream boards. Tell them everything you're learning about your money sabotages and ask about their financial history too.

Donna says, "My husband's mother has real issues around money. She'll ask how much we pay for everything and it's really embarrassing. She was a widow, raising three boys on a pension and obviously had to count every penny, so it rubbed off on my husband.

"He will automatically say *'we can't afford that'* no matter what it is, so it's difficult to make First Class upgrades."

Donna's husband wasn't even aware of his language or how his childhood affected him and was at first extremely reluctant to acknowledge it. Donna had to sit down and have a stark heart to heart about what the impact it was making on their shared money experience. Now they call each other on their negative language and she can lovingly ask him to stop saying things like "we can't afford that".

Shared dreams manifest so much quicker when two

people focus their energy in the same direction. I've seen it many times in my life, especially when Mark and I used our powers together to win the Ultimate Job travel competition.

If you feel like your family environment isn't supporting your highest good, which sometimes happens, even with married couples, you need to stay strong and know where you're going. I've said to my own husband, "This is my vision for our life. I'm going there no matter what. I'm going there with you or someone else. I really hope it's you, because I love you, but if it's not that's fine. I'm going on this train no matter what. So you're either on the train or you're off the train".

Luckily, he took that really well and he wanted to be on the train. Whew! Sometimes now I'm a bit of a bitch about it. If we're having an argument, I'm like, "Dude, are you on the train or are you off the train, because the train's leaving and I'm going to kick you off!"

Doing this work together can make your relationship stronger and then you have a true partner on the path to wealth creation.

On the other side, I've seen many women who have upgraded their thinking so much that they just don't vibe with their partner anymore and it ends. It's sad but it's always for your highest good.

Look at everyone in your life and figure out whom you are bumping up against for this particular income level. Work out what it is that you're afraid of and then do some clearing around it using the tools we've covered earlier.

It will be someone different at each level of wealth, so when you get stuck, think of everyone in your life who earns that level of income.

I've been in masterminds where everyone wanted to get to six figures. Once I reached it, I didn't resonate that much anymore with the mastermind. I stayed on to pay it forward and help others, but now I needed to move onto a different group where people were earning more than me, so I felt stretched. Otherwise, I might start holding myself back to not "outgrow" anyone.

Take the earlier example of Lindsay who felt uncomfortable when she started to earn more than her rich uncle. It wasn't her uncle who was holding her back. In fact, if she asked him, he probably would have only been incredibly encouraging. It was Lindsay's own thoughts that put her in that place, not his. She needed to take responsibility for that before she could move on and be comfortable with a higher income level.

And guess what, you'll find someone else to "blame" next time!

Krystal says "In my first round of the Money Bootcamp, I identified my dad as my major energetic saboteur, as I thought it was unseemly to earn more than him. Clearing that was unbelievable and my income went up almost immediately. After four months, I knew that I had hit my next income ceiling.

"It took me a while to figure out who the next person was, but after pushing past six figures in my business, I realised that my first coach, a woman I really respect and admire had hit her own income ceiling and had plateaued for a few years. It suddenly felt awkward knowing I had surpassed her in income. It felt icky and Denise's favourite word 'unseemly'. I cleared it and forgave myself for earning more than her. I had to let myself realise at a cellular level that it was safe to be richer than her, it didn't mean that I disrespected her in any way. Clearing that allowed me to add another 10% to my income quickly."

Isn't it funny, how we keep ourselves small?

Fear of Being Seen as a Snob

One of my clients, Cassandra, was in a mentally and emotionally abusive marriage where her ex-husband used to tell her that she was a snob because she went to a prestigious university. He had her convinced that everyone thought she was a hoity-toity bitch because of her upper-class schooling, even though she had won a scholarship. Because of this she had to down-play her education and accomplishments. Her husband had his own issues around not going to college, so to make himself feel better, he would make his wife feel bad. He was taking her power away.

For Cassandra this hugely impacted her wealth consciousness and she deliberately held herself back in her business, so she didn't shine brighter than other people in her industry. She had the bitch fear too!

"I've been called bossy. I know that I'm the type of person who doesn't have to be the leader, but if people aren't going to be good, I'll feel like telling them to get out of my way, so I can show them how it's done," said Cassandra.

We're afraid that, when we stand up in our power, like Cassandra, other people will not like it. We have all experienced this in some way, either with family, our friends, or in our relationships.

Find light in the beautiful sea
I choose to be happy
You and I, you and I
We're like diamonds in the sky
Rihanna

Success, power and money go hand in hand. When you show up powerfully in your life, the money will follow. That doesn't mean that only strong and confident Alpha women can be rich. You can be powerful and quiet. You can be introverted and you can be a show-off if you want. The point is, money is attracted to clarity and when you are confident in yourself and know where you're going, the Universe will reward that.

How many weak and hesitant CEOs have you seen? The most successful people in this world are those who had the courage of their convictions to stand up and do something they believed in. Their confidence then encouraged others to follow them, buy from them and work for them.

There was a great Pantene shampoo advertisement in the 80s that said: *"It won't happen overnight but it* will *happen"*, so keep on making those empowering upgrades, even if those around you seem uncomfortable with the changes in you. You're not doing it for them so who cares what they think – you're doing this for you.

While you are upgrading your life and taking back your power, find others that support you and the changes you are making for the better. Connect with women who are going where you want to go, because they will not call you a bitch; they will not call you bossy; they will not call you a snob. They will only celebrate your accomplishments.

Dealing with Haters in Business

When you are in business for yourself and you get your first hate mail, I see that as something to celebrate, because it means you're reaching more people and there's always going to be some people who don't like you. Seriously, send me a tweet to @denisedt and say "I got my first hater, woohooo!"

There is usually 3% of people in your life or business who will love you to the point of stalking and will buy everything that you create. These are your biggest fans and it's incredibly flattering to be loved and admired.

The next 20% of your audience *like* you, maybe they even love you a little bit. Then you have a whole bunch of people in the middle who are completely ambivalent to you.

Then you have another 20% of people who kind of don't like you that much.

Then you have the last 3% of people who will always freaking hate you! Everything you do will annoy them and they'll go out of their way to bash your reputation, send you nasty emails and be the biggest pains in the butts ever. The only way to deal with those people is to block and delete. Don't engage, don't try and make them like you. Just let them go from your world. Don't read your hate mail. Just delete it.

In our normal life, we just don't know that many people for the percentages to play out, but when you live bigger and become a leader, you stick your head up above those tall poppies, and suddenly more people know who you are. You can't focus on the 3% of people who hate you, who think you suck, or who think your way of life is terrible. You have to just turn your attention to the 3% of people who love you, and the majority of the people who like you.

I'm fine with criticism, because it just doesn't affect me as much anymore. I know that some of that is a rite of passage of playing bigger in the world.

It's pointless to say to the Universe, *"Send me success, send me money, but I don't want a* single *person to dislike me or call me bossy or a bitch"*.

It's like asking to win the lottery. The combination of things that the Universe needs to put that together for you is too complex, so it could take ages to manifest. Just focus on creating your abundance and accept the rest as a slightly negative consequence of success.

When people are judging you as a bitch or aggressive or anything negative, it's really about them. They're not comfortable within themselves and your behaviour is threatening to them. Remember, you're not responsible for other people's crap so don't take it on.

Jealousy is Normal

What if *you're* the one who isn't happy for others and you're pissed that other people are lucky and abundant?

When jealousy rears its ugly head, it is a perfect sign that someone has something that you want for yourself. Yes, it sucks, but you can take it as a message from the Universe: *"I hear you and it's ready for you if you want it. Just to prove it, I'm going to bring it into your awareness"*. The Universe is showing you it's ready and available for you if you are ready to claim it for yourself. Otherwise, it will manifest through someone else to remind you.

I get jealous all the time, but I've found a way to create something amazing from it, and you can too. It can actually be a great manifestation tool because it shows you what's possible for yourself.

At one stage in my late twenties, I was so frustrated with myself that I was still working in a cubical and not being the millionaire I envisioned myself being by age 30. I really wanted to be made redundant from my job, because I didn't want to be there, but I wasn't ready to quit either. I just wanted *something* to happen. Anything to get me out of there.

All of a sudden, two of my close friends were made redundant and had massive financial payouts. One friend got a six month tax-free payout and the other friend got 18 months. I just remember thinking, *"Are you kidding me? That's what* I *want! Universe, why did you give it to* them *and not me?!"*.

I was soooo jealous, much worse than the Christmas when my brother got a camera that *I* had actually asked Santa for. I was not happy for my friends. I was *sick* with jealousy. It came at the perfect time for both of them, they had no families to support and they were suddenly free and cashed up for fun and travel.

I asked my friends how they were going to spend their money and all the while I was thinking, *"You lucky bitch. This sucks. Why can't someone just pay* me *to not work and go travelling? Why can't that happen to me?"*. I was pretty pissed off until I realised that I couldn't manifest from a place of jealousy. It had obviously happened to teach me something and it gave me a swift wake up call. What if nobody gave *me* a payout or made me redundant? Was I willing to stay stuck forever? How long was I willing to wait for my windfall?

That's when I decided to set some really clear goals and take responsibility for my own life changing experience. I wanted to go travelling for six months, and I wanted to work for myself *no matter what*. If someone gave me a payout, that would be great, but I was done with staying still and hating my life.

Every time that jealousy came up, I put my hand on my heart and affirmed, "*Good things are happening to me too*". It got me through that crippling jealousy and got me out of the story that only good things happened to other people. Not coincidentally, it sparked off probably the luckiest time in my life. More on that in a second.

I'd love to say that I'm an incredibly generous person and I'm always 100% happy for others, but it's not true. Generally I am, but when I experience jealously, it's a clear sign that I need to get clearer on my goals.

When Gabby Bernstein published her second book and then got on Oprah? Grrrrrr.

When my friend Michelle lost ten pounds and looked incredible in a bikini? Bitch!

When my friend Leonie bought a huge big house and had a record month in her business? Omg, that sucked for a few days and then I pulled my big girl panties up and hustled my butt off. She was actually a huge inspiration for us to move into the penthouse.

It's actually a great thing if you're jealous of somebody you know because you can see first-hand how they do it (you can even just *ask* them) and when you see it, you're more likely to believe it for yourself.

So, experiencing jealousy right now? That's an amazing sign that you're going to the next level in your life! All my clients know my favourite affirmation and if you're experiencing jealousy at the moment, try this one.

Hand on heart:

"It's my time and I'm ready for the next step."

By doing this you can transform that jealousy into the rock-solid belief that something amazing is just around the corner for you too.

You can also look at it as a little test from the Universe. Think of the Universe showing you a menu with pictures: *"Is this what you are looking for? Is this what Madam would like?"*. Just because it's manifesting in your friend's life, doesn't mean you can't have it too. There's more than enough abundance to go round.

That's exactly what happened to me. When I transformed my resentment of my friend's windfalls into appreciation and acceptance that good things could happen to me too, *guess what happened*?

It was only a few months after that I won the round-the-world honeymoon competition. Someone did actually pay me for six months to do what I loved. When my friends called me a lucky bitch, I smiled and told them that good things were happening to them too.

Surround Yourself With Wealth-Minded Women

Chances are your friends have vastly different ideas about money and life. Maybe some of those friends are having a hard time adjusting to the new more confident and abundant you.

I've experienced this. I've had people in my life I loved dearly, but being friends with them started to feel a little bit like an obligation because I knew they weren't coming along with me on my journey.

It doesn't mean that all of your friends have to be exactly like you and have the same level of ambition. You're not a bitch if you want to have more like-minded friends.

Because, to be honest, if you want to be really successful you have to surround yourself with other successful people. It's not enough to have a mentor, although I think this is awesome.

You have to have people at all levels around you who are living life at that same vibrational frequency of success and abundance. Everyone you are with on a day-to-day level, your friends, your success team, your partner, needs to be lifting you up not dragging you down with obligation, negativity and poverty mindset.

I'm not going to sugar coat it. Sometimes you might need to take a break from some friendships if they are getting you down. Usually when this happens you will start to meet more like-minded people who can help you have a rich mentality.

As well as a coach who helps me get to where I want to go, I have an amazing group of women who help and support each other. We all have six figure businesses, with dreams of becoming million dollar business owners. It's the sort of group where you can share a massive dream and they'll understand and support you.

In contrast, you might be surrounded by women who complain all the time that life is against them, every month is a drama to pay their bills and play the victim game all the time, "Why is this happening to meeeee?". It's not fun and you don't have to put up with it.

Limit the time you spend in their negative energy, hide them on your Facebook wall and change the subject when they bitch about their life. They probably won't change, so you have to limit your personal exposure. (Please don't send them my way, I can't "fix" anyone). If you have to see them, go to the movies together. That way you limit the amount of "bitching time" and enjoy a nice movie together (especially if it's a Ryan Gosling movie - he fixes *everything*).

Oh, and of course, forgive them and send love to their journey. You can still love them and choose not to be around them anymore. It's okay.

It's weird but sometimes people will go out of your life without you consciously making the choice. It's like your energy just doesn't align anymore.

I experienced this a few years ago. I had a friend who constantly called me to bitch about her job. I just couldn't relate anymore because I was successfully building my business and most of my friends were entrepreneurs, not frustrated employees. After a few of those phone calls, I asked her *"Well, what are you going to do about it?"*. She was taken aback at first. I think she just wanted to continue the old pattern where she moaned about her inability to change anything and expect sympathy. I just got bored of it and snapped. I then said to her, *"This seems to be a recurring pattern in your career, what are you learning from it?"*. This *really* sent her over the edge, but it's just like the clichéd bad boyfriend syndrome. At some point, you can't keep enabling your friend to make the same mistake over and over again. You don't *have* to listen to it.

This new assertive Denise wasn't appreciated by my friend who accused me of having no time for her anymore and told me she didn't like "the person I'd become". I thought that was sad because I liked myself for the first time in ages, and although I still love her, I'm relieved not to have daily phone calls anymore because that energy really bummed me out.

Throughout doing my Money Bootcamp course, many of the participants find the same thing happening. They stop tolerating friends who sabotage them, perpetuate their negative stories about money or make them feel bad for wanting a bigger life.

Amanda says: "My friend actually called me a snob when I went to try on clothes in a fancier store than normal. She said it jokingly and before the Bootcamp, I would have laughed and agreed with her, but instead I said "Okay, wait outside for me". She was completely shocked and was standoffish for the rest of the afternoon. In hindsight I realised that since we were friends in high school, I've played second best to her in every way. We went where she wanted to go, she set the trends and she had to be the centre of attention."

Amanda has a choice to make. Keep her life the same to avoid upsetting her friend or break away and do what *she* wants to do. It's okay to want to be the star of your own life and it's not high school anymore. You don't have to follow the queen bee or be the same as anyone else.

You might think, "Well, *who* would I be friends with then?"

Me for a start!

I'm building a virtual army of amazing women from all countries and all walks of life. Together we can talk about money, get excited about hitting our goals and support each other through the next milestone. Trust me, you won't be lonely!

Walking away from your friends might seem scary at first but you could actually look at it from a positive angle. It's not like you're dramatically breaking up with them (although that sometimes happens), you're just crowding out any form of negativity in your life. Think of all the new friends you can make. You can start to be really choosy with the people you hang out with. Choose friends who will lift you up to new levels of abundance, not drag you down to their level of poverty thinking.

If you're making this big change to find new friends in your local area, join some hobby groups, maybe a singing or a sports team. You could even arrange a meet up with other people in your industry and not only treat it as a friend finding mission but also a networking opportunity. You could also take some education classes and meet like-minded people. Join some of my Lucky Bitch online programs to meet amazing women who are changing the world by changing their abundance mindset. You can be the first to know by signing up to my exclusive newsletter at www.LuckyBitch.com.

Thank the Universe for the wonderful people in your life and stay positive and smile and in no time you will start to attract some amazing new friends.

Chapter Summary

- You alone are responsible for how you feel about money
- Don't let other people's opinions hold you back from being rich
- Jealousy is a great sign that you're ready to move on
- Surround yourself with women who love to talk about money and success.

Action - tweet me and tell me about your first hater!

$

Raise Your Prices

"We do not "make" money. We create and open pathways to the flow of the energy of money."
Dyan Garris

When I work with women on raising their prices, I ask them "what would be the most *unseemly* amount of money for you to make?"

I love the word "unseemly" here, it's entirely appropriate because there is an income level for you that will feel... icky. This is where resistance starts to pop up for many women. You get to a certain income level and then the guilt factor starts to kick in and you worry that people will think it's inappropriate for you to earn that large amount of money.

I've hit that unseemly amount many times. It's not actually real, nor is it actually inappropriate, it's just an excuse for you to experience a temporary energetic income barrier and you can use that feeling to break through it to the next one. I remember one barrier very clearly.

"I don't wake up for less than $10,000 a day."
Linda Evangelista

I was starting to do some speaking engagements and had no idea what to charge, so I'd just ask them what their budget is. Whatever they said was their budget is what I said my fee was!

So, I got this speaking gig for $500 and I was so excited to tell my mum about it. Now, speaking can pay thousands of dollars, but I was pretty chuffed with my $500, until I told my mum.

My mum is an assistant nurse who works really hard for her money. As I told her about the speech, I started to think, "How many shifts would she have to work to earn $500?". I felt really embarrassed and it suddenly felt kind of obscene to earn that money for 45 minutes of enjoyable work.

You might have the same thing, whether it relates to someone you know or about the world in general, "*How can I earn money so easily when there are starving people in the world?*". That kind of thinking will keep you stuck at the same income level for years and doesn't serve you anymore.

I felt the same when I put my prices up, which I do regularly and encourage my clients to do the same. This one time, I announced my prices were going up, but the problem was I hadn't committed to a new price. That's because I started to feel bad about my awesome job. What would people think if I earned shit-loads of money to sit around in my yoga clothes, talk to people about their life, and be paid really good money for it? In my mind, I thought "Who am I to make that kind of money?"

Have you ever thought;
Who do you think you are?

Who am I to charge that?
Who am I to out-earn everyone in my family?

It's so common for women to put unconscious limits on how much they are "allowed" to earn. That's why this work is ongoing as you'll hit the same issues at different income points. You'll get through one, then get the urge to increase your prices again and think, "Oh no that's way too much for me to earn. That really is unseemly now!"

I love seeing people repeat my Bootcamp and push through what they thought was possible, so be prepared for a life-long process as you become even richer.

"I make a lot of money, but I don't want to talk about that. I work very hard and I'm worth every cent."
Naomi Campbell

I had several months this year that was my best income level ever and each time I said to myself, *"Well, that's just a fluke. There is no way I can do that again. There is no way I can replicate that"*.

Guess what? The next month was even better but that little voice was still there, "Now this really is a fluke. How can I possibly beat it for next month? There's no way". How did I get rid of this self-defeating voice? I forgave myself and I did some EFT around it. I realised that it wasn't just a fluke, but my hard work and efforts were actually paying off. That's why I move quickly, I'm constantly decluttering and asking myself what's holding me back from the next level.

Rachel increased her income over four weeks by $10,000, but she was having trouble telling her father about her success. Growing up she had always seen her father work really hard and long hours to make a living. He was rich but worked 18 hour days in stark contrast to Rachel who drastically increased her income without having to do too much more work.

"My dad worked his arse off and I grew up with the idea that life wasn't meant to be all roses," Rachel said.

It turned out that Rachel's dad was her barometer in life of how good she could have it, and how success could show up. She cleared that belief that if she eclipsed her dad in happiness or success without burning herself out she would be a horrible daughter.

Don't let them be your excuse. Remember it's your thoughts that determine your income, not your loved ones.

Affirmation:

"My family wants great things for me and is proud of my success."

If you feel like you need to moderate yourself or pull back a bit from your dreams because it's just a bit too much, or if that guilt is starting to kick in, take a look at where in your life have you heard that before? Did your parents teach you that it's not good to have too much? Were they content with just enough?

Maybe you were taught that having ambition was a bad thing, it made you unfeminine or ruthless.

Go back to the forgiveness work and the EFT to help clear those crappy self-beliefs so you can be, do and have everything you've ever wanted.

"Even though I'm too ambitious, I deeply and completely love and accept myself."

How to Choose Your New Income Level

While I was thinking about raising my prices and bumping up against my own bullshit resistance, I did an exercise with my business coach to test out my next energetic income level. At the time my prices were $300 per session and even though I had started out at $75 and had increased every few months, I knew it was time to stretch myself again.

We did an energetic exercise where I closed my eyes and she asked me to think of different prices, *"Okay, what feels right? Is it $350? Is it $400? Is it $450? Is it $500…?"* And she just kept on going. At some point I said, "Oh no that's too much" and we took it down a little bit and that's where we settled, at $550. It felt good to do that. We worked out the turning point where I started to feel too uncomfortable and stopped there. The new price still felt like a stretch but I reached my new energetic income threshold.

Try it for yourself. Sit with your own energetic income levels or get a friend or your coach to ask you. Keep pushing yourself until you find your next price or income goal. It should feel like a stretch but in an exciting way.

It's got to be congruent though. I once set a really big stretch goal but I could feel myself chickening out. I realised that all my passwords were all different. Some of them were my exact income goal, others were fifty or even a hundred thousand dollars difference. From a law of attraction perspective, what message does that send to the Universe?

Conversations around prices rises are common among female entrepreneurs. You can't base your prices off what other people in your industry or environment charge. Why not? Because you're using *their* energetic income barriers as the basis for your own! A lot of female entrepreneurs have massive resistance to earning money, so don't use them as your barometer. It's okay to be the most expensive and to challenge conventions to what's possible.

Most coaches in my area charge $75-$150 per session, so already I'm breaking convention. You really can charge what you like if you're offering a service that people want, especially if you have an online business, you can find clients all over the world and target countries that have a great economy.

You can decide to be the best at what you do and get paid accordingly. My kinesiologist is really awesome at what she does, she's the best. But she is also booked out all the time, because her prices are pretty low for the results she gets for her clients. I told her I would pay double to be able to see her when I wanted. Her response was that nobody would pay it. I would!

Don't have assumptions to what people can pay you. I've assumed people can't pay for coaching and then I find out they're really wealthy. If you believe you are surrounded by broke people, you'll only perpetuate that with your client base.

It's also relevant if you're an employee; think of raising prices in terms of asking for a pay increase. Do this exercise to test the levels of what you would be comfortable with earning, because if you're not an energetic match, then you'll manifest the situation where your boss doesn't see it either. It explains why I never earned much in my corporate career, despite having some awesome jobs, my boss just reflected what I felt on the inside about my self-worth.

You can do it for yourself now, by writing down your current income or salary. If you have your own business, write down what you've made this year to date.

Now add 10% to that. Just sit with it for a moment. Sit with it and look at that number. How does that number feel? Does it start to bump up against your own energetic income level?

Just see whether there are any little voices that come up and say things like:

Nope, that's not for you.
You're not smart enough to earn that.
Your clients will think you're a bitch.
Nobody charges that much.
Your boss would think you're being demanding.
You'll go broke and lose all your clients.
That's too extreme, nobody would pay that much.

Just see what comes up for you if your prices or income increased by 20%. How does that feel?

Now, look at that number again and double it. Imagine that is your income. How does that feel? For some people, it might cause an immediate reaction in your body. Your heart might start to pound. You might get short of breath and start to freak out. You might get a little tingle of excitement with a *hell yeah!*

You might think, "How the hell am I going to do that?". That's not your job right now to figure it out. Your only job is to *dream it.*

Keep going and double it again. And again.

Can you imagine that it's possible? Can you imagine what would be different in your life with that income? Can you imagine living an absolutely First Class life?

Every single time you increase your prices or ask for more money, there will be a new income level where you'll start to think, "Well, that's just too much. Nobody needs that kind of money. What would I do with all of it?"

"Somebody said to me, 'But the Beatles were anti-materialistic.' That's a huge myth. John and I literally used to sit down and say, "Now, let's write a swimming pool."
Paul McCartney

No More Bartering

Giving away services for free seems to be a recurring theme with entrepreneurial woman. I know I have done it before and always regretted it. When you barter instead of getting paid for your work, you devalue yourself as a business woman and don't show the Universe you're making money a priority.

I made a commitment in my second year of business that I wouldn't do any more bartering (exchanging products or services with someone else) and it changed my business.

I used to barter even though I didn't really want to because I didn't want to say no and have people think I was being a bitch. I decided to start saying no to these sorts of request for discounts and for free things just to see what happened. It's been amazing because people have been like, "Hey that's okay, no harm in asking!". By doing this I took back my power in my business, after all it's my business so I have the right to choose how I run it.

When you raise your prices, you have to be energetically consistent and not exchange your services with other people anymore. It gets to a point where you deserve to make *real* money for the work you do. It's part of being able to receive more and it's a strong sign to the Universe that you're ready to be paid what you're worth.

When I made that initial commitment, I had several people email me and ask if they could do my Money Bootcamp for free. Of course, it was just a test from the Universe! I have to admit, I still hated saying no to people, but I did it with grace. You can even blame me and say it's part of your *Get Rich, Lucky Bitch* assignment!

As soon as you make the decision, your income will increase. You'll have more opportunities to make more money and no longer align yourself to people who need a handout. If you still want to give things away and feel powerful, organise a scholarship for your program.

Megan, who coaches woman to be healthy and lose weight would get up to a couple of hundred emails a day with requests for help from women. In the past she had always answered each and every one and while some turned into paid clients, many didn't, and she would end up doing free consultations with them. The endless back and forth of emails was eating up much of Megan's time and energy without any payoff, and sometimes not even a thank you!

What I advised Megan to do with these types of emails was to send a reply basically saying "Thanks for your email, it sounds like you could do with some coaching, here's the link to my webpage".

"While it was a scary step to make, it was actually very liberating!" Megan said.

By being upfront in turning down requests for free help you can save yourself huge amounts of time and energy, and still remain professional.

People who are really serious about wanting your help won't mind paying for it. And by showing the Universe that you believe your services are worth paying for, you will start to attract more clients that believe that too and are happy to pay you for your services.

"You are taking control of your money because doing so will make you feel happier and smarter, more confident, more content, and more useful."
Jean Chatzky

Can you make a commitment from here and now, no more discounts, no more bargaining and no more bartering?

Affirmation: It's safe for me to be rich.

What would you spend the extra money on? It could be travel. Why not travel in style or even just more frequently? Extra money may bring you peace of mind and financial security. Maybe you can pay off your mortgage. Or maybe for you it's about being able to help other people. Having more money means you can give more to charity. You can give some to your family. You can support causes that mean a lot to you. You can build the most environmentally friendly house in the world, you can sponsor dog shelters – hell, you can bathe in money if you want to – no judgement here!

Money is just an energetic tool and how much you manifest is completely up to you.

I asked Paula Muñoz, one of my Money Bootcamp

participants what life is like for her now.

"I feel so grateful. I have been literally feeling that right now my life could be described as 'ask and it is given'. Two days ago I said to the Universe I needed cash and the day after I found 250 euros out of the blue. I said to the Universe I needed to buy organic olive oil because I am running out of it and my in-laws brought us a five litre bottle from their trip. I said to the Universe we needed to buy a hoover for our new apartment, I even put it in my be, do, have list for the next six months calculations and we received an industrial hoover that nobody uses anymore from my boyfriend's family. I said to the Universe I needed a kitchen clock and I found one in the box room. The list goes on and on and on... I am waiting for the HUGE stuff to manifest now. I know for sure it's on the way! Thanks Universe, thanks Denise and thanks bootcamp!"

Life seriously can be that easy when you increase your energetic income level and allow yourself to receive.

"Money has no power other than that which we give it."
Jim Stovall

Overcoming Income Resistance

No matter how many goals you set, no matter how motivated or ambitious you are, don't blame yourself if you feel like you are bumping up against that energetic income ceiling again. It could come after a period where everything felt amazing and money flowed to you like crazy.

The good news is that you have everything you need

in this book to break through it. The bad news is that eventually you'll hit the next ceiling.

Every single time I raise my prices, it's really scary. I worry that nobody will pay them, that someone will send me an email saying *"Who do you think you are missy?"*. However, after a couple of months it feels normal and then I get that familiar itch to raise them again. It's not being greedy, it's that you get better at what you do and you should be able to command higher prices for the value you offer in the world.

Stuck at One Income Level for Ages?

Income resistance feels real because each time that evil little voice that says *"This is really it now. This is the most you'll ever earn"*, it really sounds like it knows what it's talking about. It doesn't.

You should raise your prices or ask for a pay increase every six months. At the *very minimum* once a year. If you work for yourself, you could raise your prices on your premium service every quarter. Look at your product funnel to ensure you have a mix of entry level, affordable and most importantly leveraged products and you have a premium priced exclusive and expensive product or program. You never want to be known as the cheapest in your industry. Undercutting everyone else is not a quick or fun way to become rich.

When you hit your new income resistance, you might start to talk yourself out of everything on your goal list as "unrealistic" or "unnecessary". It's not unusual to do that, so don't worry. You'll probably downgrade your big income goal to something less scary. You might even go back to old habits and buy economy items again like cheap toilet paper or scrimping on travel. You'll get a whole bunch of temptations like clients asking for discounts or people asking for loans. Recognise your pattern of RSI and stay strong in everything you've learnt so far.

This is a normal part of the process and everyone goes through it. After experiencing the pleasure of the upgrade, you'll only do that a few times before you learn, trust me baby!

Being Comfortable with Excess Money

So many of us are so uncomfortable with having too much, we do everything we can, consciously or not, to reduce it.

Excess just means "more than you need" and we've been conditioned to be okay with just the minimum. And how you do one thing is how you do everything. When you get comfortable having more money than you actually "need", you become wealthier, but you have to deal with this at an energetic level. That's when you turn excess into abundance.

A while ago I realised the reason why I could never save money is because I was uncomfortable with having excess food.

What's the connection? If there was food on my plate, I had to eat it all, even if I felt uncomfortable. It felt naughty and bad if there was even a scrap left on my plate because of the "starving children in Africa". So I often over-ate as a form of body sabotage.

I realised that I was the *exact* same way with money. If I had money in my purse, I had to consume (spend) it all. I didn't feel comfortable energetically unless I spent *every* single cent in my account by the end of the month. Even when I went shopping, I'd keep going until there was no money left, even if I had to spend my last five dollars on a smoothie.

I felt guilty if I had more than I actually needed, so energetically, even if I saved money, I would manifest an unexpected expense so I ended up at square one again. This is one of the most common things I see working with women. They feel guilty if they have "spare" money lying around and they feel like they should give it to others or consume it as quickly as possible.

That way, even when some people raise their prices, they increase their expenses just as much so it doesn't make that much of a difference.

I had to train myself to get comfortable with having more money than I needed. Then magically, the same thing happened with my food. I became okay with saying, "I'm done", and pushing it away. Whether it's with money or food, it's really healthy to start becoming okay with abundance.

If you find it hard to save, see where else in your life you are uncomfortable with excess. If you are uncomfortable with having more than you need, that is going to have a huge impact on your ability to save money. Maybe you feel bad if someone gives you a present out of the blue or your husband buys you flowers "just because".

Start a Savings Account Now

Have you ever got really gung ho about saving and then something unexpected comes up and you have to "raid" it?

I have been saving money regularly for a while now and it's amazing. I haven't raided it the whole time because like the incremental upgrade, I started small and got more comfortable with larger amounts. I literally started with saving five dollars a week. Even though I was earning good money and I kept raising my prices, I was weirdly scared to save it. So I did forgiveness on myself for spending so excessively in the past and did EFT on the fear;

Even though I won't have enough money if I save some, I deeply and completely love and accept myself.

When I realised that I never even missed the five bucks, I upped it to $7, then $15, then $22, then $33, then $50 and now I save $200 a week. It still might not sound like a lot, but I was so uncomfortable with the excess that I had never, ever in my life been able to save money before.

Try it today. Set up a really small amount of money, one that you won't miss and it won't trigger your sabotage at all. Every two months, increase it by another tiny amount.

The "Save and Never Spend" Syndrome

Some women are the complete opposite. They are brilliant at saving money but it never feels *enough*, so they are terrified at spending it and ending up poor. So they squirrel it away and never enjoy it. The extreme of this is the little old lady who lived in poverty but gave millions away in her will.

If this sounds like you, examine why you don't like spending your money, is it because you think you don't deserve it? Are you worried that you'll be broke if you spend a little bit of the money? Maybe you're a reformed shopper who has swung the other way in extreme.

There's nothing wrong with having a huge amount of savings in the bank, but I'm going to encourage you to spend *some* of it. Like the incremental spending, take a small percentage of your income, say 5% that you *have* to spend on pleasure, Denise's orders! Increase that over time so you're spending at least 10% of your income on things that make you feel amazing.

Set a savings goal and have an emergency fund in case something should happen. That way you can feel safe and once your savings goal is fulfilled, you can practice treating yourself. Remember, it's not about buying the most expensive, it's your version of a First Class life. You could get pleasure out of buying solar panels for your house or the most luxurious sequinned high heels ever. Nobody can tell you how to spend your money, as long as it gives *you* pleasure.

Chapter Summary

- It's safe for you to earn more than others
- Allow yourself to receive money and say no to bartering, no matter what
- Income resistance is normal, you'll break through them one at a time
- Start saving and being comfortable with excess money

$

Rearrange the Universe in Your Favour

"The world is more malleable than you think, and it's waiting for you to hammer it into shape."
Bono

It's awesome when you're on fire and money is manifesting all over the place! Welcome to the world of the Lucky Bitch.

Now, let's take it one step further. If you're still reading this book, I know you're serious about creating more wealth in your life.

Making big commitments, being serious about them, and following through on your promise with real-world actions will show the Universe you are dead serious about wanting to manifest more money and that you are ready to take your life to the stratosphere of what is possible.

This is what separates the "rah rah" personal development junkies and people who *actually* manifest amazing success in the real world. Positive thinking will only get you so far; now you gotta hustle girlfriend!

I don't really believe in luck by itself. I believe you have to grab life by the reins and steer it in whatever direction you want to go.

Your Next Big Commitment

I really see success as made up of hundreds of commitments over time. Each time it will feel big and scary then it will be no big deal. That's why it has to be something that stretches you. Otherwise, the Universe is like "meh". Ditto with getting rich. You have to set realistic but slightly scary goals regularly so you can experience your wealth over hundreds of wins. That way you won't be a millionaire overnight and lose it all buying a private jet or something stupid that you can't really afford.

Make your commitment to raise your prices now

Make a big commitment that will have an immediate impact on your income, like raising your prices by next month, launching a new program or announcing a sale.

The best way to make it stick is to make a *public* commitment - put it on your website or newsletter and figure out the details later. If you wait til you feel "ready", it will never happen and you're just deluding yourself. The more public you make it, there's less chance you'll back out. Yes, you might still have a momentary freak out and get scared but you can just push though.

I'm a big fan of 'fake it til you make it' because you'll be surprised how much other people take it as face value. People will believe you. The more people you tell about your commitment, the more the belief compounds and then you just move forward automatically without thinking about it.

This always astounds me. When I started writing

books, I had to *force* myself to tell people I was an author. I didn't believe it, but the more I said it, I could see that other people believed me. People started asking me when my next book was coming out, and I was like, "Wow, they really think I'm a real writer".

Taking action towards your goals, no matter how small will help you believe it's possible. Just move forward "as if" it's happening.

If your dream is to buy a house, go and see a mortgage advisor and get your financing done. The financial advisor will believe you that you want to buy a house, will run the numbers and tell you how much you can borrow. Faced with that *real* number, you go and tell a real estate agent you're buying a house and they will believe you too! Go to open houses and you'll start to believe you're buying a house.

All these small actions help you act as if you're someone who's really buying a house. You start to tell your friends and family that you're buying a house – they tell you their stories about when they bought a house and they freakin' believe you too! Before you know it, you're buying the house, but if you never make that series of small commitments you'll be forever sitting in your old house by yourself with it all happening in your head. Get it out of your head and into the real world.

Your commitment can't be some vague time-wasting action like "research". It has to be something that rips a hole through time and space, or even something that pokes a hole in it and involves other people. This includes public commitments and test driving your dream life.

Pony Up and Put Down Some Dollars

I love playing Texas Hold 'Em and especially for cash. I don't have to pay a lot of money to enjoy it, even five bucks will keep me concentrated on my cards. But if I'm just playing "for fun", I'll bow out early, get distracted by T.V. or my phone and take smaller risks. I literally have no investment in winning.

You have to put some skin in the game and that's the best commitment of all. Put down that non-refundable deposit on the holiday, conference or training course and you'll move heaven and earth to manifest the rest of the money. Wait until it falls from the sky before you commit and you'll probably lose the chance.

I was talking to Janelle, an awesome young entrepreneur who was frustrated about increasing her coaching prices. She told me she was attracting time wasters and people who tried to haggle her all the time. She knew she wanted to price herself higher than her competition and her branding definitely reflected that - she was seriously talented, but something wasn't gelling. I asked her the most amount of money she'd ever spent on a course.

She told me "about a hundred bucks, but I hardly ever spend money on courses. I usually try and do a barter arrangement to get it free".

Um.

Yep.

I lovingly pointed out that if she had never experienced paying for a premium priced course herself and always bartered, chances are she'd attract people with the exact same vibration. You have to be in congruence to your goal and you can't ask your clients to do something that you don't fundamentally believe yourself. There's an energetic mismatch and they *feel* it.

I knew that I had to move house if I wanted to move into a bigger income level. Our last apartment was small and cute but it wasn't a millionaire's house. My office was the spare bedroom that was supposed to house two single beds. To fit in my desk, we piled the beds on top of each other. So the back of my office chair touched this huge mound of mattresses. Pretty hard to manifest a million dollar business in that kind of space, right? Even though my clients couldn't see it, they could energetically feel it. It was a mismatch to my premium pricing.

Now I'm working from my penthouse overlooking the harbour with my own dedicated office. The building is also home to at least one millionaire. Again, even though my clients can't *see* it, don't you think they can *feel* the abundance through my energy?

You have to invest in yourself for the Universe to invest in YOU.

Chapter Summary

- Fake it until you make it, the Universe can't tell the difference and neither can your brain!
- Make sure you have some skin in the game
- Tweet me your big commitment to @denisedt

$

How to Manifest Money Quickly

"When you let your money move to things you care about, your life lights up.That's really what money is for."
Lynne Twist

How do you manifest money quickly for something you really want to do? Easy!

This is a really simple process I do every time I want to manifest money for conferences and events. This works for anything you want to find money for quickly, but I developed it when I had just started my business and my hubby expressively forbad me putting another personal development conference on our credit card. So, I set about manifesting it.

Say for example you wanted to attend a personal development conference in New York but you don't actually have the cash right now to pay for flights, accommodation, conference tickets and all the rest of the fun that goes along with a trip. Don't despair, you can create the money really quickly. I've done this when I wanted to go to conferences in Vegas, New York, Dallas and Tucson and it always works if you follow the steps.

I've won the money, been given tickets out of the blue,

had unexpected tax refunds and came up with creative ideas to earn it. But I've always used the same practical process which is about simply living, speaking and behaving as if you are no-joke, 100% going to go to that conference, so the Universe gets the message loud and clear that you're not just randomly entertaining the idea, you are going *no matter what.*

First thing, before you start freaking out about the money, schedule it in your calendar. It's completely free and will take 10 seconds to block out the event (plus travel time) into your calendar. Be generous and allow yourself space to get to the event on time and without stress, as if everything is going to rearrange itself for you. *Do it now*.

By scheduling it, you're making it real and you create energetic space for the event. You might find there's a calendar clash you have to take care of, but at least you can take action now and avoid the drama later. You'll also get your first test to see if you really want to go. Oh no, you'll have to miss the season premiere of *The Walking Dead* or a fabulous party. Do you still really want to go? YES? Ok, moving on…

Next, start making your apologies for anything you'll miss while you're away. Cancel or reschedule your clients. Ask someone to cover for you or take notes at your class for you. Switch around your long-standing hair appointment. Make life easy for yourself now and clear any physical, emotional or energetic clutter from you being there. Every time you do this, the other person will simply believe that you're going without question, so don't say "I *might* be in New York", just declare it as if it's already a forgone conclusion. This will help your resolve. I've had clients rearrange their husband's or even their mother in law's birthdays once they realised there was a clash. This really is the first test to see if you actually want to go.

Remember, you can't manifest just by *thinking* about it because it's easy to chicken out, so involve other people in this manifestation. This builds in multiple layers of accountability and you can't be vague about it. You are GOING to that damn conference (or holiday or ski trip, whatever it is).

The next step is to write a list of the expenses. Write out your wish list to Santa with the cost of everything you need; event admission, travel costs (don't forget transfers), food, accommodation, spending money, merchandise, alcohol, visa costs, snacks, etc.

Now remember, you're a lucky bitch so don't get all cheap on yourself. I know what you're doing. Don't write out the minimum costs for how you could scrimp and save to be there.

Be generous with your request to the Universe, because you never know you might manifest the money to the penny, and you'll be bummed you didn't ask for more!

I like to include a hair appointment for every trip (so I don't have to take my hair straighteners or products, plus I can sleep in AND look like a million bucks = triple win), and prefer to get a taxi or a car than a cheap shuttle bus. I love buying a new journal for each conference and a couple of awesome pens.

Don't budget to stay offsite, a million miles from everyone else - get the best room you can afford at the event hotel. You don't want to stay in some budget flea hole while everyone else is staying onsite at a gorgeous location. There's nothing worse than being in an awesome city but not having enough money to enjoy it.

So far, you're just speculating and dreaming, you haven't had to pay any money yet, but see what's coming up for you. Are you starting to freak out, second guess yourself or feeling guilty about spending the money? Are you trying to be el cheapo with yourself, justifying how little you could spend on the trip?

I was at a conference last year, having dinner on the outside patio looking out into the desert with two lovely women. One is my mastermind buddy, so we have awesome conversations about money all the time. The other woman was reading through the menu and stressing about the price of everything - she wouldn't even buy herself a glass of wine. She said that every night after the conference, her and another woman were driving to the local McDonalds to eat instead of the gorgeous restaurant.

I remember those days well.

I've stayed in some horrible places, stressed about every cent and missed out on some awesome fun. So, please add a realistic but generous figure down on your letter to Santa!

Next, start taking real-world action.

This means you should RSVP for the event, buy your ticket, or tell the organiser you'll be there. Enquire about the travel arrangements. Make sure your passport is up to date. Arrange a baby/dog sitter. Hell - start packing if you want!

Even if the money hasn't materialised for the entire trip yet, book your hotel NOW. You usually only need to give a credit card number to confirm and most hotels usually don't charge it before your stay. You probably have a standard 24-48 hour cancellation policy, so there is no risk but it feels like a real commitment, even though it doesn't cost you anything. Put the hotel confirmation number in your calendar entry.

Don't forget to ask the event organisers if there is a special event room rate for a group discount. Join the hotel reward program. Get the best room you can afford, organise with a friend to share a room or let others know you're looking for a room-mate.

I've recently started booking two room suites for myself, even if I've got nobody to share with. I did this in New York and ran a small group workshop which paid for the hotel room = total win! Another time, the upgraded room got me free entry into a special club lounge which included free breakfast, pre-dinner drinks and canapés, plus complimentary clothes pressing. The more expensive room ended up saving me tonnes of money, as I ate every meal in the club lounge (like it was an all-you-can-eat buffet). The point is, the Universe always rewards you when you reward yourself. Rich people know this.

I've also been so cheap with myself that it ended up costing me even MORE money. The "cheap" hotel room is miles away from anywhere so you spend extra on cabs, the "free" shuttle bus takes forever and you miss your flight or you just end up feeling stressed and poor because you had to watch every penny. I hate arriving somewhere all sweaty and stressed because the traffic was bad or the free shuttle bus had to pick up every random in town.

Figure out what else you need to organise for your trip and pre-book that too, starting with whatever you can afford now, even if it's just pre-paying for the hotel shuttle or the conference drinks party. I usually book my hair appointment online, organise lunch with a friend and sign up for pre-event activities too.

Don't forget to buy the VIP ticket option. Often it's just a bit more expensive but you get food included or you get to meet the speakers. It's worth every penny and you'll meet other people who also invest in themselves who could end up being great mastermind buddies or even joint venture partners. You want to pay to be surrounded by other wealth conscious people. Make sure you join the pre-conference Facebook group or contact the organiser on social media to say how excited you are about attending.

Why go to all this trouble? Every action is highly symbolic (even if it costs you nothing), and each new commitment is bringing you closer to actually being there. If you have no skin in the game, it's unlikely you'll move heaven and earth to be there, but if you've committed to another person or company, you won't want to let them down.

It's weird but the thought of losing a $20 pre-booked shuttle might make you more determined to find the rest of the money. You won't want to tell your room mate she'll have to find someone else because she'll be pissed. You'll make it happen. You'll start to believe you're actually going, because many other people just assume that you'll be there.

I almost backed out of several conferences while I was in the process of manifesting money except for the fact I'd be letting down my room-mate. The thought of that kept me hustling to ensure I'd be there.

At some point in this process, you'll start to receive some temptations and tests from the Universe to see if you really want to go. Someone will ask you to speak at an event, invite you to a cool party or an "important" family commitment will come up. Maybe you'll get sick or there'll be unexpected expenses, like that dreaded tax bill or a speeding fine.

Trust me - this always happens, so just smile and recognise it for what it truly is. The Universe is just testing if you really want to go, so avoid temptation to fold or let the doubt creep in. Remember - you're going, no matter what. It's in your calendar, right? (If not, take two minutes and book it in now. I'm highly serious about this).

Okay, so you get an awesome invitation to speak at a local conference or your friend's impromptu back-yard wedding. Here's where you have to be firm and reinstate your intention not only to the Universe but to people around you. Just calmly say "I'm sorry, I can't - I'm going to be in New York then", as if you totally are (because you totally will be!). This is a strong declaration to the Universe and saying no always gives you the extra power to make it happen.

Soooo, you're doing all this and the money STILL hasn't shown up? By now, you probably will start to see a little trickle, so make sure you resist the temptation to use it for something else. Example - you get an unexpected $50 and instead of being all like "Whoo-whoo, a cool fiddy bucks towards New York!", you start to backtrack... "I really should use this for the credit card/Tommy's new shoes/dental bills". Remember that chapter on guilt?

Yes, all of that is important and you shouldn't ignore important or urgent things for the sake of your trip. However, unexpected money is a gift from the Universe and you should allocate all or a certain percentage towards your trip. Otherwise you're pushing away abundance that the Universe sent you for a reason.

The final step is to hustle and make it happen no

matter what. Yes, an unexpected cheque might come in the post, but don't leave it to chance, because the more effort you put in, the more the Universe will meet you half way.

Think laterally about how you can generate the cash and I recommend making a list of 20-50 things you can do to make money. Keep going with new ideas even if they are redonkulous. List things that you wouldn't *really* do, like baby sitting or selling your grandma's china unless you were really desperate but the act of writing them down, shows that you're willing to make it happen no matter what you have to do.

Here are some ideas for you:

Announce a sale on your products
Email that potential client you've been putting off
Sell some clutter on eBay
Sell old books on Amazon
Get your tax refund organised
Ask for cash for your birthday
Chase up expense claims at work
Submit insurance or health claims

Tell your friends and family you're going. You never know, someone might gift you with some spending money! This has happened to my clients on numerous occasions, because once you've started the flow of money, you can't really turn it off.

Print out the details of your trip or the conference itinerary and visualise yourself being there, travelling on the plane and meeting new friends. Feel that tingle of excitement in your belly and practice saying "I did it!". Imagine yourself telling the story of how you manifested the trip. Imagine sending me an email telling me how you did it. Never ever give up. It will work.

This kind of process can be applied to any situation such as a holiday, personal development event, education course or even a really fabulous expensive meal at a fancy restaurant. The main thing is that once you start really believing that you are going and you are living in the reality where you are going to do the course, take the trip or visit the restaurant, the Universe will help you get there.

Every time you practice this process you'll get better and better, but here's the truth:

The money won't show up until you commit to going – not the other way around.

It really does work. Here's a story from a bootcamp participant:

"I found an old bank book that said it had £900 in it - I had no idea if it was still open so I wrote to close it and got a transfer of £1200! I'm thrilled as it paid for a course that I committed to doing. This is the second time that I took a leap and the money showed up. Thank you Denise." - Claire Wade, Money Bootcamp participant.

If you're just wishy washy about it, you'll never consciously manifest the money. You have to commit first and move forward no matter what.

Chapter Summary

- Follow the steps: put it in your calendar, commit to going, tell people you're going book everything you can, put some money down, tell others you'll be there, make a hustle list, allocate money to going and you'll get there!

Bonus - get my free video on how to manifest money in 24 hours! Sign up at www.GetRichLuckyBitch.com with password LOVEMONEY

$

Money Loves You

"Why you? Because there's no one better. Why now? Because tomorrow isn't soon enough."
Donna Brazile

It was sooo hard to come to this final chapter. This book felt like it would never end, not because of procrastination but because there was *so much* I wanted to share with you about creating amazing abundance in your life. OMG, can't we just hang out together forever?

I really hope that reading this book has inspired you to start making some big changes in your life and in the way you deal with your money. I hope you are well on your transformational journey to becoming a wealthy woman.

I want to leave you with a few last thoughts on continuing your success and keep growing into the woman you were meant to be.

Anchor In Your New Money Experience

I love celebrating and anchoring in successful experiences and I believe that my income has increased quickly because I've celebrated every milestone. When you applaud yourself for every success, you anchor that experience into your subconscious and attract even more success.

Remember my first $225? I actually bought myself a bottle of champagne because I wanted to send a clear message to the Universe that I was proud of every single cent and I expected that more was on its way.

Never stop learning and growing, but when amazing things happen, take a moment to anchor in the experience, feel the *weight* of it and don't be afraid to ask for more.

I'm sending over my sincerest congratulations and acknowledgement for everything you're doing in your life. I know you're working hard to create an incredible life for yourself.

Success Breeds More Success

One thing I've learnt is that making money gets easier and easier. You'll discover this for yourself as you get richer.

The more evidence you have that you are successful the easier it will be to attract more of the same. I would love you to commit to celebrating over the next couple of days, the successes that you've been able to bring into your life through changes you've made around money. Total up every single cent of extra money you've brought in from reading this book and say to yourself, *"I'm really proud of you, babe. Well done"*. Celebrate your new energetic income level!

You are Exactly Where You Need to Be

If you feel like you haven't achieved everything that you wanted to by this stage in your life, don't worry, you're exactly where you need to be right now and you found this book for a reason.

You might feel like you should be doing things quicker, doing more forgiveness work, manifesting more money and be further along in your journey.

The problem is, when you feel like that, you're *always* going to feel like that. You're always going to feel like you're a step behind. Put your hand on your heart and affirm out loud,

"I'm exactly where I'm supposed to be. It's my time and I'm ready for the next step".

You're Never Going Back

It's easy to get excited when you learn a new personal development tool or discover a new author, but once the hype wears off, you're the same as before. Let's make a commitment together that this is a *permanent* change for you and you're never going back to how you used to be with money. Never.

It's okay to love money, because money loves YOU!

No matter what, I want you to know that the Universe does love you and money just wants to take care of you.

It's okay to love money. To talk about it, invite it to play with you and enjoy spending it. Now that you are part of a global network of Lucky Bitches, you are never alone. You can admit to us that you love money and you can even brag to us that money loves YOU.

"I WANT to enjoy money. I want to like money. I want to like having *money. I want to like touching money. I want to like getting money and spending it. I want to FEEL good about money. I want to have more money than I know how to spend. I want to be able to feel exhilarated when I think of money."*
Bernadette Wulf

Be Rich, Don't Try to Get Rich

Don't try get-rich-quick schemes. It honestly never works. I really hope you use the information in this book to create amazing things in the world with your new wealthy mentality. It starts with the decision that you *already are rich.*

It really can be that easy.

You Can Choose Your Own Adventure

Never forget, your future is entirely up to you. There are many different financial realities that you could choose and there are so many different possibilities for your life, each one just as real as the next.

Imagine that each of these future possibilities is an individual bubble. Each one contains a different version of you. Rich, poor or every shade in between. You can choose which path and which journey you take in this lifetime. Just choose the bubble that looks the most appealing and step into it! (That makes an awesome meditation by the way!)

I promise, that if you follow just some of the lessons in this book you will become richer in spirit *and* in your bank account.

Your First Class life is out there waiting for you, and

by making all those little upgrades and becoming the VIP you were born to be, you are going to get closer every day to your First Class life.

Just by reading this book your financial makeover has begun.

Yes sometimes it won't be an easy ride, and of course your path will have ups and downs, but believe that your success is inevitable and it will be, you lucky bitch!

I can't wait to hear all about it,

Xx Denise
www.LuckyBitch.com

P.S. Can you do me a favour? If you loved this book, please share it with a girlfriend. We have to spread the word and create a whole planet of abundant Lucky Bitches who are changing the world.

$

Success Stories

It's one thing for me to go on about how easy it is to manifest the life of your dreams but it's another thing to hear from those who are actually starting to manifest things they desire. I've included the following stories to inspire you and show you just how much you can transform your life in a short amount of time. All these women have done my Money Bootcamp course. It's a practical six week online course where we put into practice many of the ideas in this book, plus much more. We go deeper into the concepts around the Law of Attraction and I am on hand throughout the course to help you take your life to the next level.

If you want to find out about my next bootcamp go to www.LuckyBitchBootcamp.com

"I never realized how much emotional baggage in my life was connected to money and earning potential. The limitations were all literally coming from within me, and working through the coursework in the Lucky Bitch Money Bootcamp helped me to realize just how much power I had to change all that!

Now, I say "thank you" more – to people and to God and the Universe. I smile more because I know that staying in a positive mood and frame of mind will attract more positive things into my world.

I love working with Denise because she's NOT all fluff – she's action-oriented and great at helping me to get focused, all the while working together to release all the money drama from my past to keep me thinking about all the great things that I'm manifesting for my future."

– Melanie Ramiro, *Speakers Agent and Photographer.*

"My biggest money block was not believing that I could take my income to the next level. It was like I had decided the place where I was at was perfectly ok, and I didn't need to stretch myself any further.

It took me to go through the lessons to really believe that it IS possible to manifest what you want. I wanted to win a photo competition I'd entered for a free holiday to Sri Lanka, so I just started tapping (which I'd never done before the Bootcamp) and visualising and manifesting my little heart out, and just kind of felt in my heart that I would win – and I did!

I also had an amazing moment when I listened to Denise's subliminal money mantras recording, and literally while I was listening, I attracted a new client and received payment for something unexpected – it was exciting, weird and freaky, all at the same time!

I now have the confidence to go forward with my business, with the belief and understanding that I can be successful."

– Simone Samuels, *Holistic Health Coach.*

"I had my biggest month ever in my business earning over $4000 on my first ever e-course and having 25 women sign-up with a wait list for the next course! I have less limits and blocks around my business and earning money from it. I can't explain it, but it just unblocked me and allowed me to move forward into my business and I can see the amazing success ahead of me.

Denise's course helps you to move past your blocks, let go of the fear and just go out and be fabulous! There is a lot of ACTION in this course which really pushed me forward and I am so grateful. If you're feeling a connection with this course but are sitting on the fence, do it, be open to it, and just allow yourself to grow and expand with it!"

- Kathryn Hocking, *Business Coach.*

"For the first time in my life, I'm doing it. I'm making money. Signing up to Bootcamp was terrifying; I've never spent that amount of money on an e-course before. But deep down I knew I needed to do it, that if I didn't invest in changing my attitude to money then I'd always be stuck in that place of never fulfilling my potential. And I'm so glad that I took the risk. Outstanding monies that I was owed from work I'd done a couple of months before turned up in my bank account on day 1 of the Bootcamp (all £1000 of it!), which made me laugh; it seemed like a very good sign that I was doing the right thing!

Money Bootcamp has changed my life, it's that simple. You read statements like that in testimonials, but the reality doesn't sink in. I can't emphasize this enough, I am a different person than I was two months ago. I am building a career as a creative, marketing myself and networking, growing in confidence day by day. I'm demanding that I'm treated with respect as a professional. I'm challenging the belief that creatives can't make money. I'm determined to be both creative and financially savvy. I now believe in myself. And I'm loving it!

If you've always felt held back in life and don't know why, take this Bootcamp. If you know deep down that you're not fulfilling your potential, take this Bootcamp. If you've never had any money (or can't hold on to it), take this Bootcamp. If you're ready to tackle the underlying causes of why you're not enjoying the success you deserve, take this Bootcamp. It will help move you forward, without drama, without complaining, without spending five years in therapy. Decide today that you want life to be better and start investing in yourself. It works."

– Katherine Mitchell, *Writer.*

"I think that at the root of it all I was scared of money. Scared that I'd never have any. Scared what I'd do with it if I did have some. Scared what would happen if I made it and then it all went away. Scared.

During the course the biggest surprise was the ideas that would quite literally hit me over the head during the day. Way to make money or get out of my own way so I could receive money (yes, filing taxes would be a good idea, wouldn't it?!). Money suddenly wasn't so mysterious.

Now, I'm less reactive about money and far more proactive. Knowledge is power and knowing how much money you actually have and how much more you need to reach your goal is power.

Denise is sweet, supportive and incredibly understanding. I couldn't recommend her more highly as a coach."

- **Parisa Roohipour,** *Singer-Songwriter, Artist, Yoga Teacher.*

"During the 6 weeks of Lucky Bitch Money Bootcamp, I manifested an $800 scholarship to a personal growth worth shop in Maui, picked up 3 new clients for my business, and $1,210 in unexpected income for the month. Next, I asked that I sell my house within two weeks of putting it on the market. We got an offer three days later for $5,000 more than we asked for it! Now I am feeling great and fully embracing the abundant life that has been waiting for me to show up.

Even my boyfriend tonight said, "You have been making money in such strange ways, I can't believe it." I said, "Believe it babe, I am one lucky bitch!"

Now that I sold my house, I paid off my debt, I have a better vision of what I want my life to be like, and I have $100,000 in the bank if I want to put a down-payment on another house. I have decided that there is no reason I can't create the exact life I want, so I am really going for it with my business. I am so excited to be focusing my time, love, and attention on what I care about. I am so stoked!

YOU are the best investment, YOU are the most valuable thing you can invest in. Keep on believing, you are so worthy and deserving of the best life possible. Create it now!'

- **Stephanie Dodds,** *Holistic Nutritionist, Raw Foods Chef, Blogger.*

"I was a complete mess when I joined the first boot camp. I felt very dependent, insecure and just like a failure.

Now I live my dream life. I enrolled in a coaching certification seminar and already started working and have paying clients! I love what I do and I know I am on the right track and I live my purpose in life

I am so happy that I did the boot camp. So grateful for the community Denise created! These girls are the best! My life is not the same anymore...so grateful!"

– Alla Petcheniouk, *Spiritual Life Coach.*

"Exactly six months after completing my first round of Bootcamp, I manifested and closed my first VIP client (their investment is over five-figures) without putting any elbow grease into marketing this high ticket service -- they 100% came to me. Unreal!

I had NO idea about the stories that I have been telling myself for years. Denise really helped me dive really deep into points of reference in my life that have really shaped the way that I look at things. Her Money Bootcamp was seriously life changing. I will never look at money the same again. And as I continue to stay involved with each new round of Bootcampers, my realizations become deeper and I literally become richer. I can't thank you enough, Denise.

Money does not overwhelm me anymore -- it is a true miracle!"

– Aimee Prezzano, *Simple Living Consultant for Busy People.*

"I felt like I was stuck at one income level and that no matter what I did I couldn't earn any more. I seemed to have a lot of fears around money. I also wanted to help get my husband back in sync in the way we thought and talked about money after he was retrenched and had three months out of work.

I set a money goal for the first month of Bootcamp that was 50% higher than any previous month - and achieved it! My other big goal was to pay off my credit card in full - which I did by the end of the course.

Now, my husband and I have upgraded lots of things and our money related conversations are really positive."

- Kerry Belviso, *Kinesiologist.*

"During the Bootcamp, I was pleasantly surprised to win a ticket to a huge life changing event. We also received an unexpected $1000 after the Bootcamp finished. Another thing that happened was a lot of people unexpectedly offered their help to fix our garden which saved us lots of money... I also got a great editor for my book that cost the exact amount I was visualising."

- Anna Garcia, *Life Coach and Graphic Designer.*

$

Join Me in the VIP Lounge

Today is your lucky day!

I'd love to invite you to join a global community of women changing the world by embracing outrageous success and claiming the title of "Lucky Bitch".

Here's how to play:

1. Sign up to get your free Get Rich, Lucky Bitch bonuses and you'll also get my weekly inspiring newsletter, with exclusive surprises just for my Lucky Bitch posse, so make sure you're on the VIP list here, (the password is LOVEMONEY) www.GetRichLuckyBitch.com

2. Love this book? Manifested something awesome? I'd love to hear from you! Please email your manifestation stories to info@luckybitch.com

$

About Denise Duffield-Thomas

My serious business lady bio

Denise Duffield-Thomas is a coach and motivational speaker who helps exceptional women create outrageous success. Her book "Lucky Bitch" is a practical and fun take on the Law of Attraction and what it really takes to manifest your wildest dreams.

Denise holds a Business Studies degree and after university was a global coordinator for AIESEC International, based in London. Professionally, Denise has worked for PricewaterhouseCoopers, boutique consulting firm Future Considerations (favourite client, the United Nations) and for children's charity Barnardo's before winning the Ultimate Job competition, a six months all expenses paid blogging gig for an Irish honeymoon company.

Now the CEO of LuckyBitch.com, Denise runs mindset training programs for women, consults female entrepreneurs and travels the world attending and speaking at conferences.

Denise lives in sunny Newcastle, Australia with her husband Mark Duffield-Thomas.

Random facts about me

Together with my husband Mark, we attempted a Guinness World Record attempt for most married couple; we've been married 87 times in over 12 countries including with a Masai tribe, with sharks at the Great Barrier Reef and at the Waldolf Astoria, NYC.

In case you're curious about my name – I was Thomas, he was Duffield. Together we are Duffield-Thomas, although I wanted us to create our own unique name like Tomfield or Duffas.

I performed as the Sydney Olympic mascot Millie the Echidna for two years leading up to the Sydney games, including the closing ceremony.

My top 5 strengths: Futurist, Learner, Intellection, Achiever and Ideation. My Fascination Advantage type is Avante Garde and I'm a Virgo with an incredibly messy desk.

I'm pretty lucky but I'm not much of a bitch.

My passion in life is helping other women live incredible lives.

Xx

Denise

www.LuckyBitch.com